Dat...
Illur...

CATHERINE M. RIC...
Iona College

D1471417

JONES AND BARTLETT PUBLISHERS
Sudbury, Massachusetts
BOSTON   TORONTO   LONDON   SINGAPORE

World Headquarters
Jones and Bartlett Publishers
40 Tall Pine Drive
Sudbury, MA 01776
978-443-5000
info@jbpub.com
www.jbpub.com

Jones and Bartlett Publishers Canada
2406 Nikanna Road
Mississauga, ON L5C 2W6
CANADA

Jones and Bartlett Publishers International
Barb House, Barb Mews
London W6 7PA
UK

ISBN: 0-7637-2692-3

Printed in the United States of America
08 07 06 05 04   10 9 8 7 6 5 4 3 2 1

Contents

How This Book Can Help You Learn

All of us have different learning styles. Some of us are visual learners, some more auditory, some learn better by doing an activity. Some students prefer to learn new material using visual aids. Some learn material better when they hear it in a lecture; others learn it better by reading it. Cognitive research has shown that no matter what your learning style, you will learn more if you are actively engaged in the learning process.

The Student Lecture Companion will help you learn by providing a structure to your notes and letting you use all of the learning styles mentioned above. You don't need to copy down every word your professor says or recopy your entire Computer Science textbook. Do the assigned reading, listen in lecture, follow the key points your instructor is making, and write down meaningful notes. After reading and lectures, review your notes and pull out the most important points.

The Student Lecture Companion is your partner and guide in note taking. Your Companion provides you with a visual guide that follows the chapter topics presented in your textbook, *Databases Illuminated*. If your instructor is using the PowerPoint™ slides that accompany the text, this guide will save you from having to write down everything that is on the slides. There is space provided for you to jot down the terms and concepts that you feel are most important to each lecture. By working with your Companion, you are seeing, hearing, writing, and, later, reading and reviewing. The more times you are exposed to the material, the better you will learn and understand it. Using different methods of exposure significantly increases your comprehension.

Your Companion is the perfect place to write down questions that you want to ask your professor later, interesting ideas that you want to discuss with your study group, or reminders to yourself to go back and study a certain concept again to make sure that you really got it.

Having organized notes is essential at exam time, when doing homework assignments, or when working on programming problems. Your ability to easily locate the important concepts of a recent lecture will help you move along more rapidly, as you don't have to spend time rereading an entire chapter just to reinforce one point that you may not have quite understood.

Your Companion is a valuable resource. You've found a wonderful study partner!

Note-Taking Tips

1. It is easier to take notes if you are not hearing the information for the first time. Read the chapter or the material that is about to be discussed before class. This will help you to anticipate what will be said in class, and have an idea of what to write down. It will also help to read over your notes from the last class. This way you can avoid having to spend the first few minutes of class trying to remember where you left off last time.

2. Don't waste your time trying to write down everything that your professor says. Instead, listen closely and only write down the important points. Review these important points after class to help remind you of related points that were made during the lecture.

3. If the class discussion takes a spontaneous turn, pay attention and participate in the discussion. Only take notes on the conclusions that are relevant to the lecture.

4. Emphasize main points in your notes. You may want to use a highlighter, special notation (asterisks, exclamation points), format (circle, underline), or placement on the page (indented, bulleted). You will find that when you try to recall these points, you will be able to actually picture them on the page.

5. Be sure to copy down word-for-word specific formulas, laws, and theories.

6. Hearing something repeated, stressed, or summed up can be a signal that it is an important concept to understand.

7. Organize handouts, study guides, and exams in your notebook along with your lecture notes. It may be helpful to use a three-ring binder, so that you can insert pages wherever you need to.

8. When taking notes, you might find it helpful to leave a wide margin on all four sides of the page. Doing this allows you to note names, dates, definitions, etc. for easy access and studying later. It may also be helpful to make notes of questions you want to ask your professor or research later, ideas or relationships that you want to explore more on your own, or concepts that you don't fully understand.

9. It is best to maintain a separate notebook for each class. Labeling and dating your notes can be helpful when you need to look up information from previous lectures.

10. Make your notes legible, and take notes directly in your notebook. Chances are you won't recopy them no matter how noble your intentions. Spend the time you would have spent recopying the notes studying them instead, drawing conclusions and making connections that you didn't have time for in class.

11. Look over your notes after class while the lecture is still fresh in your mind. Fix illegible items and clarify anything you don't understand. Do this again right before the next class.

Notes

Databases Illuminated

Chapter One
Introductory Database Concepts

Uses of Databases

- Used in large and small organizations. Examples
  - Consumer websites—ordering products
  - Customer service websites – e.g. utility, health insurance, telephone service providers
  - Online banking
  - Credit card companies
  - Supermarkets and retail stores, including inventory control systems
  - Airline reservations
  - Medical records and billing
  - Employment records
  - School records
  - Bibliographic databases

A Sample Database

- Simple University database
- Need to keep information about
  - Students
  - Classes
  - Professors
  - Enrollment-links students to their classes
- Example uses Microsoft Access
- Data represented as **tables**
- Each row of Student table represents one student
- Each row of Class table represents one class
- Each row of Enroll represents **relationship** between one student and one class

See Figure 1.1

Query Tool

- Microsoft Access has a simple tool for forming and executing queries
- Query: Find the names of all students enrolled in ART103A
- Need to use Enroll table and Student table, since Enroll does not have names
- Figure 1.2 shows query result

Reporting Tool

- Microsoft Access has a report generator
- Example: Print a report showing each class number, the ID and name of the faculty member teaching the class, and the IDs and names of all the students in that class
- Figure 1.3 shows the report

The Integrated Database Environment

- **Database**
  - Large repository of data
  - Shared resource, used by many departments and applications
  - Contains several different record types
  - "knows" about relationships in data
  - Managed by database administrator - DBA
- **DBMS**, Database Management System
  - Controls access to database
  - Has facilities to
    - Set up database structure
    - Load the data
    - Retrieve requested data and format it for users
    - Hide sensitive data
    - Accept and perform updates
    - Handle concurrency
    - Perform backup and recovery ... and many other functions...
- **Users**
- **Applications**

Example of Integrated Database Environment

- See Figure 1.4
  - University database
  - DBMS - may be Access, Oracle, DB2,...
  - Users may be individuals on workstations (interactive users) or application programs
  - Both users and applications go through DBMS
  - Applications produce standard output, such as reports

People in Integrated Database Environment

- End users
  - **Casual users** use query language
  - **Naïve users** use programs
  - **Secondary users** use database output
- Applications programmers – write programs for other users
- Database administrator (DBA) – designs, creates, maintains the database
- See Figure 1.5

Advantages of Integrated Databases

- Compared with file systems, database can provide
  - Sharing of data
  - Control of redundancy
  - Data consistency
  - Improved data standards
  - Better data security
  - Improved data integrity
  - Balancing of conflicting requirements
  - Faster development of new applications
  - Better data accessibility
  - Economy of scale
  - More control of concurrency
  - Better backup and recovery procedures

Disadvantages of Databases

- Compared with file systems, databases have some disadvantages
  - High cost of DBMS
  - Higher hardware costs
  - Higher programming costs
  - High conversion costs
  - Slower processing of some applications
  - Increased vulnerability
  - More difficult recovery

Brief History of Information Systems -1

- Early human records-clay tablets, hieroglyphics, cave paintings, paper records of family histories, treaties, inventories, and so on
- Hollerith used **punched cards** in 1890 US census
- **Punched paper tape** introduced in 1940s
- **Magnetic tape** introduced about 1950-used in UNIVAC I
- Cards, paper tape, magnetic tape are **sequential access devices**
- Used in sequential processing applications such as payroll, shown in Figure 1.6
- **Batch processing** uses master file and transaction file as input; produces new master file as output

Brief History of Information Systems - 2

- Magnetic disk introduced in 1950s - **direct access device**
- Programming languages COBOL and PL/1 developed in 1960s
- Early database models developed
- Hierarchical model
  - IBM IMS developed for Apollo moon landing project
  - IMS product released in 1968
  - Most popular pre-relational DBMS
  - SABRE airline reservation system used IMS
- Network model
  - GE IDS developed by Charles Bachman in early 1960s
  - CODASYL DBTG proposed standards published in 1971
  - ANSI rejected proposal
  - New standards published in 1973, 1978, 1981 and 1984
  - Provided standard terminology, notion of layered database architecture

Brief History of Information Systems-3

- Relational model
  - Proposed by E.F. Codd in 1970 paper, "A Relational Model of Data for Large Shared Data Banks"
  - Strong theoretical foundation
  - System R, late 1970s
    - IBM's prototype relational system
    - Introduced SQL, Structured Query Language, now standard language
  - Peterlee Relational Test Vehicle at IBM UK Scientific Laboratory
  - INGRES at University of California, Berkeley
  - ORACLE used some System R results
  - Early microcomputer relational DBMSs :dBase, R:Base, Foxpro, Paradox
  - Microsoft Access most popular microcomputer-based DBMS
  - Oracle, DB2, Informix, Sybase, and Microsoft's SQL Server most popular enterprise DBMSs

Brief History of Information Systems-4

- Entity Relationship model
  - P.P. Chen, 1976
  - Semantic model – tries to capture meaning
- Object-oriented model
  - Can handle complex data
  - Introduced in 1990s
- Object-relational model:object-oriented capabilities added to relational databases
- Data warehouses developed in 1990s
  - Take data from many sources
  - May store historical data
  - Used for **data mining**, finding trends in data
- Internet provides access to vast network of databases
  - E-commerce
  - Wireless computing
  - Thin clients such as PDAs

Notes

Databases Illuminated

Catherine Ricardo

Databases Illuminated

Chapter 2
Database Planning and Database
Architecture

Data as a Resource

- Resource: an asset that has value and incurs cost
- Resources include capital equipment, financial assets, personnel **and data**
- **Database** is a resource because
  - Operational data has value
  - Database incurs cost
  - Professionally managed by DBA

Characteristics of Data

- Data vs. information
  - Data: raw facts
    - Example: printout of tables as they are stored
  - Information: processed data, useful for decision-making
    - Example: formatted report using database

Four Levels of Data

1. Real world
   - **Enterprise** in its environment
   - **Miniworld**, or **Universe of Discourse** – part of the world that is represented in the database
2. Conceptual Model
   - Entities, entity sets, attributes, relationships
3. Logical model of database
   - **Metadata**, data about data
   - Record types, data item types, data aggregates
   - Stored in data dictionary
4. Data occurrences
   - Database itself
   - Data instances
   - files

Data Sublanguages

- Every DBMS uses a data sublanguage, which has two parts
  - **Data definition language (DDL)** - used to define the database
  - **Data manipulation language (DML)** - is used to process the database
  - Data sublanguage may be embedded in a general programming language (such as Java, C, C++, C#, COBOL, and so on) which is called the **host language**

Staged Database Design

- **Systems analysis** approach to design assumes every system has a **lifecycle**, and will eventually be replaced
- **Staged database design** centers on first developing a **conceptual model** that evolves and survives

Characteristics of a Conceptual Database Model

- Faithfully mirrors the operations of the organization
- Flexible enough to allow changes as new information needs arise
- Supports many different user views
- Independent of physical implementation
- Does not depend on the model used by a particular database management system

Stages in Database Design

- Analyze user environment
- Develop conceptual data model
- Choose a DBMS
- Develop logical model, by mapping conceptual model to DBMS
- Develop physical model
- Evaluate physical model
- Perform tuning, if indicated
- Implement physical model

See Figure 2.3 – note loops

Design Tools

- **CASE** (Computer-Aided Software Engineering) tools
  - **Upper case**: used for collecting and designing data, designing logical model, designing applications
  - **Lower case**: used for implementing the database, including prototyping, data conversion, generating application code, generating reports, testing
- Data dictionary
- Project management software

Data Dictionary

- Contains **metadata**
- Can be **integrated** (part of DBMS) or **free-standing**
- Useful for
  - Collecting information about data in central location
  - Securing agreement on meanings of items
  - Communicating with users
  - Identifying inconsistencies – synonyms and homonyms
  - Keeping track of changes to DB structure
  - Determining impact of changes to DB structure
  - Identifying sources of/responsibility for items
  - Recording external/logical/physical models & mappings
  - Recording access control information
  - Providing audit information

Project Management Software

- Tools to help plan and manage projects, especially those with many people
- Include several types of charts and graphs
  - GANTT chart- See Figure 2.12
  - PERT chart
- User specifies
  - Scope and objectives
  - Major tasks and phases
  - Task dependencies
  - Resources, including personnel
  - Timelines
- Software can
  - Generate calendars
  - Produce graphs with different views of project
  - Provide means of communication for staff

Database Administrator Skills

- DBA must be
  - Technically competent
  - Good manager
  - Have excellent interpersonal and communication skills
- Has primary responsibility for planning, designing, developing and managing the operating database
- Database designer may do conceptual and logical design;DBA does physical design, implementation, develops, manages system

Planning and Design Stage

- Preliminary planning
- Identifying user requirements
- Developing and maintaining the data dictionary
- Designing the conceptual model
- Choosing a DBMS
- Developing the logical model
- Developing the physical model

Development Phase

- Creating and loading the database
- Developing user views
- Writing and maintaining documentation
- Developing and enforcing data standards
- Developing and enforcing application program standards
- Developing operating procedures
- Doing user training

Database Management Phase

- Monitoring performance
- Tuning and reorganizing
- Keeping current on database improvements

Three-level Database Architecture

- CODASYL DBTG and ANSI/X3/SPARC reports proposed viewing database architecture at 3 levels of abstraction – **external, logical, internal** - each with a written description called a **schema**
- Rationale for separation of external and internal levels
  - Different users need different views of same data
  - Users data needs may change over time
  - Hides complexity of database storage structures
  - Can change logical structure without affecting all users
  - Can change data and file structures without affecting overall logical structure or users' views
  - Database structure unaffected by changes to the physical aspects of storage
- See Figure 2.5

External Level

- Consists of many user models or **views**
- Has external records - records seen by users
- May include calculated or virtual data
- Described in external schemas (subschemas)
- Used to create user interface

Logical Level

- Entire information structure of database
- "community view" as seen by DBA
- Collection of logical records
- All entities, attributes, relationships represented
- Includes all record types, data item types, relationships, constraints, semantic information, security and integrity information
- Relatively constant over time
- Described in logical schema
- Used to create logical record interface

Internal Level

- Physical implementation level
- Includes data structures, file organizations used by DBMS
- Depends on what DBMS is used
- Described in internal schema
- Used to create stored record interface with operating system
- Operating system creates physical files and physical record interface, below DB

Data Independence

- Logical data independence
  - Immunity of external models to changes in the logical model
  - Occurs at user interface level
- Physical data independence
  - Immunity of logical model to changes in internal model
  - Occurs at logical interface level

Data Models

- Collection of tools for describing structure of database
- Often includes a type of diagram and specialized vocabulary
- Description of the data, relationships in data, constraints on data, some data meanings
- Most permanent part in database architecture
- corresponds to conceptual level or logical level
- **Intension** or scheme of the database
- May change with schema evolution

Entity-Relationship Model

- A semantic model, captures meanings
- Conceptual level model
- Proposed by P.P. Chen in 1970s
- **Entities** are real-world objects about which we collect data
- **Attributes** describe the entities
- **Relationships** are associations among entities
- **Entity set** – set of entities of the same type
- **Relationship set** – set of relationships of same type
- Relationships sets may have descriptive attributes
- Represented by E-R diagrams

Relational Model

- Record-based model
- Logical-level model
- Proposed by E.F. Codd
- Based on mathematical relations
- Uses **relations**, represented as tables
- Columns of tables represent attributes
- Tables represent relationships as well as entities
- Successor to earlier record-based models—**network** and **hierarchical**

Object-oriented Model

- Similar to E-R but includes **encapsulation**, **inheritance**
- Objects have both **state** and **behavior**
- State is defined by **attributes**
- Behavior is defined by **methods** (functions or procedures)
- Designer defines **classes** with attributes, methods, and relationships
- Class constructor method creates object instances
- Each object has a unique object ID
- Classes related by class hierarchies
- Database objects have **persistence**
- Both conceptual-level and logical-level model

Object-relational model

- Adds new complex data types to relational model
- Adds objects with attributes and methods
- Adds inheritance
- SQL extended to handle objects in SQL:1999

Semi-structured Model

- Collection of nodes, each with data, and with different schemas
- Each node contains a description of its own contents
- Can be used for integrating existing databases
- **XML tags** added to documents to describe structure
- XML tags identify elements, subelements, attributes in documents
- **XML DTD** (Document Type Definition) or **XML Schema** used to define structure

Notes

Databases Illuminated

Databases Illuminated
Catherine Ricardo

Databases Illuminated

Chapter 3
The Entity Relationship Model

Purpose of E-R Model

- Facilitates database design
- Express logical properties of miniworld of interest within enterprise - **Universe of Discourse**
- Conceptual level model
- Not limited to any particular DBMS
- E-R diagrams used as design tools
- A semantic model – captures meanings

Symbols used in E-R Diagram

- Entity – rectangle
- Attribute – oval
- Relationship – diamond
- Link - line

Entity

- Object that exists and that can be distinguished from other objects
- Can be person, place, event, object, concept in the real world
- Can be physical object or abstraction
- Entity **instance** is a particular person, place, etc.
- Entity **type** is a category of entities
- Entity **set** is a collection of entities of same type
- Entity set must be well-defined
- Entity type and set definition form **intension** of entity – permanent definition part
- Entity instances and actual set form **extension** of entity – all instances that fulfill the definition at the moment
- In E-R diagram, rectangle represents entity set

Attributes

- Defining properties or qualities of entity type
- Represented by oval on E-R diagram
- **Domain** – set of allowable values for attribute
- Attribute maps entity set to domain
- May have **null values** for some entity instances – no mapping to domain for those instances
- May be **multi-valued** – use double oval on E-R diagram
- May be **composite** – use oval for composite attribute, with ovals for components connected to it by lines
- May be **derived** – use dashed oval

Keys

- **Superkey**: an attribute or set of attributes that uniquely identifies an entity
- **Composite key**: key with more than one attribute
- **Candidate key**: superkey such that no proper subset of its attributes is also a superkey (minimal superkey – has no unnecessary attributes)
- **Primary key**: the candidate key actually used for identifying entities and accessing records
- **Alternate key**: candidate key not used for primary key
- **Secondary key**: attribute or set of attributes used for accessing records, but not necessarily unique
- **Foreign key**: term used in relational model (but not in the E-R model) for an attribute that is primary key of a table and is used to establish a relationship, usually with another table, where it appears as an attribute also

Relationships

- Connections or interactions between entity instances
- Represented by diamond on E-R diagram
- Relationship **type** – category of relationships
- Relationship **set** – collection of relationships of same type
- Relationship instances – relationships that exist at a given moment
- Type forms intension; set with instances forms extension of relationship
- Relationship can have descriptive attributes
- **Degree** of relationship
  - **Binary** – links two entity sets; set of ordered pairs
  - **Ternary** – links three entity sets; ordered triples
  - **N-ary** – links n entity sets; ordered n-tuples
  - Note: ternary relationships may sometimes be replaced by two binary relationships (see Figures 3.5 and 3.13)

Cardinality of Relationships

- Number of entity instances to which another entity set can map under the relationship
- **One-to-one**: X:Y is 1:1 is each entity in X is associated with at most one entity in Y and each entity in Y with at most one entity in X.
- **One-to-many**: X:Y is 1:M is each entity in X can be associated with many entities in Y, but each entity in Y with at most one entity in X.
- **Many-to-many**: X:Y is M:M if each entity in X can be associated with many entities in Y, and each entity in Y with many entities in X (many=more than one)
- Figure 3.7 shows several representation methods

Relationship Participation Constraints

- **Total participation**
  - Every member of entity set must participate in the relationship
  - Represented by double line from entity rectangle to relationship diamond
- **Partial participation**
  - Not every entity instance must participate
  - Represented by single line from entity rectangle to relationship diamond

Notes

Roles

- **Role**: function that an entity plays in a relationship
- Optional to name role of each entity, but helpful in cases of
  - Recursive relationship – entity set relates to itself
  - Multiple relationships between same entity sets

Existence Dependency and Weak Entities

- **Existence dependency**: Entity Y is existence dependent on entity X is each instance of Y must have a corresponding instance of X
- In that case, Y must have **total participation** in its relationship with X
- If Y does not have its own candidate key, Y is called a **weak entity**, and X is **strong entity**
- Weak entity may have a partial key, called a **discriminator**, that distinguishes instances of the weak entity that are related to the same strong entity
- Use double rectangle for weak entity, with double diamond for relationship connecting it to its associated strong entity
- Note: not all existence dependent entities are weak – the lack of a key is essential to definition

ER Diagram Example

- See Figure 3.12

Notes

Databases Illuminated

Catherine Ricardo

Databases Illuminated

Chapter 4
The Relational Model

History of Relational Model

- 1970 Paper by E.F. Codd "A Relational Model of Data for Large Shared Data Banks" proposed relational model
- System R, prototype developed at IBM Research Lab at San Jose, California – late 1970s
- Peterlee Test Vehicle, IBM UK Scientific Lab
- INGRES, University of California at Berkeley
- System R results used in developing DB2 from IBM and also Oracle
- Early microcomputer based DBMSs were relational - dBase, R;base, Paradox
- Microsoft's Access, now most popular microcomputer-based DBMS, is relational
- Oracle, DB2, Informix, Sybase, Microsoft's SQL Server, MySQL - most popular enterprise DBMSs, all relational

Advantages of Relational Model

- Based on mathematical notion of relation
- Can use power of mathematical abstraction
- Can develop body of results using theorem and proof method of mathematics – results then apply to many different applications
- Can use expressive, exact mathematical notation
- Theory provides tools for improving design
- Basic structure is simple, easy to understand
- Separates logical from physical level
- Data operations easy to express, using a few powerful commands
- Operations do not require user to know storage structures used

Data Structures

- Relations are represented physically as tables
- Tables are related to one another
- Table holds information about objects
- Rows (tuples) correspond to individual records
- Columns correspond to attributes
- A column contains values from one domain
- Domains consist of atomic values

Properties of Tables

- Each cell contains at most one value
- Each column has a distinct name, the name of the attribute it represents
- Values in a column all come from the same domain
- Each tuple is distinct – no duplicate tuples
- Order of tuples is immaterial

Example of Relational Model

- See Figure 4.1
- Student table tells facts about students
- Faculty table shows facts about faculty
- Class table shows facts about classes, including what faculty member teaches each
- Enroll table relates students to classes

Notes

Mathematical Relations

- For two sets D_1 and D_2 the **Cartesian product**, $D_1 \times D_2$, is the set of all ordered pairs in which the first element is from D_1 and the second is from D_2
- A **relation** is any subset of the Cartesian product
- Could form Cartesian product of 3 sets; relation is any subset of the ordered triples so formed
- Could extend to n sets, using n-tuples

Database Relations

- A **relation schema**, **R**, is a set of attributes A_1, A_2,...,A_n with their domains D_1, D_2,...D_n
- A **relation r** on relation schema **R** is a set of mappings from the attributes to their domains
- **r** is a set of n-tuples (A_1:d_1, A_2:d_2, ..., A_n:d_n) such that d_1_ D_1, d_2 _D_2 , ..., d_n _D_n
- In a table to represent the relation, list the A_i as column headings, and let the (d_1, d_2, ...d_n) become the n-tuples, the rows of the table

Properties of Relations

- **Degree**: the number of attributes
  - 2 attributes - binary; 3 attributes - ternary; n attributres - n-ary
  - A property of the intension – does not change
- **Cardinality**: the number of tuples
  - Changes as tuples are added or deleted
  - A property of the extension – changes often
- **Keys**
- **Integrity constraints**

Relation Keys

- Relations never have duplicate tuples, so you can always tell tuples apart; implies there is always a key (which may be a composite of all attributes, in worst case)
- **Superkey**: set of attributes that uniquely identifies tuples
- **Candidate key**: superkey such that no proper subset of itself is also a superkey (i.e. it has no unnecessary attributes)
- **Primary key**: candidate key chosen for unique identification of tuples
- Cannot verify a key by looking at an instance; need to consider semantic information to ensure uniqueness

- A **foreign key** is an attribute or combination of attributes that is the primary key of some relation (called its **home** relation)

Integrity Constraints

- Integrity: correctness and internal consistency
- **Integrity constraints** are rules or restrictions that apply to all instances of the database
- Enforcing integrity constraints ensures only legal states of the database are created
- Types of constraints
  - **Domain constraint** - limits set of values for attribute
  - **Entity integrity**: no attribute of a primary key can have a null value
  - **Referential integrity**: each foreign key value must match the primary key value of some tuple in its home relation or be completely null.
  - **General constraints** or **business rules**: may be expressed as table constraints or assertions

Representing Relational Database Schemas

- Can have any number of relation schemas
- For each relation schema list name of relation followed by list of attributes in parentheses
- Underline primary key in each relation schema
- Indicate foreign keys (We use italics – arrows are best)
- Database schema actually includes domains, views, character sets, constraints, stored procedures, authorizations, etc.
- Example: University database schema
  - Student (stuId, lastName, firstName, major, credits)
  - Class (classNumber, facId, schedule, room)
  - Faculty (facId, name, department, rank)
  - Enroll(stuId,classNumber,grade)

Types of Relational Data Manipulation Languages

- **Procedural**: proscriptive - user tells system how to manipulate data - e.g. relational algebra
- **Non-procedural**: declarative - user tells what data is needed, not how to get it - e.g. relational calculus, SQL
- Other types:
  - **Graphical**: user provides illustration of data needed e.g. Query By Example(QBE)
  - **Fourth-generation**: 4GL uses user-friendly environment to generate custom applications
  - **Natural language**: 5GL accepts restricted version of English or other natural language

Relational Algebra

- Theoretical language with operators that apply to one or two relations to produce another relation
- Both operands and results are tables
- Can assign name to resulting table (rename)
- SELECT, PROJECT, JOIN allow many data retrieval operations

SELECT Operation

- Applied to a single table, returns rows that meet a specified predicate, copying them to new table
- Returns a horizontal subset of original table

SELECT *tableName* WHERE *condition* [GIVING *newTableName*]

Symbolically, [*newTableName* =] s $_{predicate}$ (*table-name*)

- Predicate is called **theta-condition**, as in s$_q$(*table-name*)
- Result table is horizontal subset of operand
- Predicate can have operators $<, <=, >, >=, =, <>$, Ÿ(AND),⁄(OR), ÿ (NOT)

PROJECT Operator

- Operates on single table
- Returns unique values in a column or combination of columns

PROJECT *tableName* OVER (*colName*,...,*colName*) [GIVING *newTableName*]

Symbolically

[*newTableName* =] P $_{colName,...,colName}$ (*tableName*)

- Can compose SELECT and PROJECT, using result of first as argument for second

Product and Theta-join

- Binary operations – apply to two tables
- **Product**: Cartesian product – cross-product of A and B – A TIMES B, written A x B
  - all combinations of rows of A with rows of B
  - Degree of result is deg of A + deg of B
  - Cardinality of result is (card of A) * (card of B)
- **THETA join**: TIMES followed by SELECT

$$A \ |x|_q \ B = s_q(A \times B)$$

Equi-join and Natural Join

- **EQUIJOIN** formed when q is equality on column common to both tables (or comparable columns)
- The common column appears twice in the result
- Eliminating the repeated column in the result gives the **NATURAL JOIN**, usually called just JOIN

$$A \ |x| \ B$$

Semijoins and Outerjoins

- **Left semijoin** A|x B is formed by finding A|x|B and projecting result onto attributes of A
- Result is tuples of A that participate in the join
- **Right semijoin** A x| B defined similarly; tuples of B that participate in join
- **Outerjoin** is formed by adding to the join those tuples that have no match, adding null values for the attributes from the other table e.g.

    A OUTER- EQUIJOIN B

  consists of the equijoin of A and B, supplemented by the unmatched tuples of A with null values for attributes of B and the unmatched tuples of B with null values for attributes of A
- Can also form **left outerjoin** or **right outerjoin**

Division

- Binary operator where entire structure of one table (divisor) is a portion of structure of the other (dividend)
- Result is projection onto those attributes of the dividend that are not in the divisor of the tuples of dividend that appear with all the rows of the divisor
- It tells which values of those attributes appear with all the values of the divisor

Set Operations

- Tables must be **union compatible** – have same basic structure
- A **UNION** B: set of tuples in either or both of A and B, written A » B
- A **INTERSECTION** B: set of tuples in both A and B simultaneously, written A _ B
- Difference or A **MINUS** B: set of tuples in A but not in B, written A - B

Relational Calculus

- Formal non-procedural language
- Two forms: **tuple-oriented** and **domain-oriented**
- Based on predicate calculus

Tuple-oriented predicate calculus

- Uses tuple variables, which take tuples of relations as values
- Query has form {S Á P(S)}
  - S is the tuple variable, stands for tuples of relation
  - P(S) is a formula that describes S
  - Means "Find the set of all tuples, s, such that P(S) is true when S=s."
- Limit queries to **safe expressions** – test only finite number of possibilities

Domain-oriented predicate calculus

- Uses variables that take their values from domains
- Query has form
  $$\{<x_1,x_2,...,x_n> \text{ Á } P(x_1,x_2,...,x_m)\}$$
  - $x_1,x_2,...,x_n$ are domain variables
  - $P(x_1,x_2,...,x_m)$ is a predicate
  - n<=m
  - Means set of all domain variables $x_1,x_2,...,x_n$ for which predicate $P(x_1,x_2,...,x_m)$ is true
- Predicate must be a formula
- Often test for membership condition, <x,y,z >Œ X

Views

- External models in 3-level architecture are called external views
- Relational views are slightly different
- Relational view is constructed from existing (base) tables
- View can be a window into a base table (subset)
- View can contain data from more than one table
- View can contain calculated data
- Views hide portions of database from users
- External model may have views and base tables

Mapping ER to Relational Model

- Each strong entity set becomes a table
- Non-composite, single-valued attributes become attributes of table
- Composite attributes: either make the composite a single attribute or use individual attributes for components, ignoring the composite
- Multi-valued attributes: remove them to a new table along with the primary key of the original table; also keep key in original table
- Weak entity sets become tables by adding primary key of owner entity
- Binary Relationships:
  - 1:M-place primary key of 1 side in table of M side as foreign key
  - 1:1- make sure they are not the same entity. If not, use either key as foreign key in the other table
  - M:M-create a relationship table with primary keys of related entities, along with any relationship attributes
- Ternary or higher degree relationships: construct relationship table of keys, along with any relationship attributes

Chapter 5: Normalization

Notes

Databases Illuminated

Databases Illuminated

Catherine Ricardo

Chapter 5
Normalization

Objectives of Normalization

- Develop a good description of the data, its relationships and constraints
- Produce a stable set of relations that
  - Is a faithful model of the enterprise
  - Is highly flexible
  - Reduces redundancy-saves space and reduces inconsistency in data
  - Is free of **update**, **insertion** and **deletion anomalies**

Anomalies

- An anomaly is an inconsistent, incomplete, or contradictory state of the database
  - **Insertion** anomaly – user is unable to insert a new record when it should be possible to do so
  - **Deletion** anomaly – when a record is deleted, other information that is tied to it is also deleted
  - **Update** anomaly –a record is updated, but other appearances of the same items are not updated

Anomaly Examples: NewClass Table

courseNo	stuId	stuLastName	fID	schedule	room	grade
ART103A	S1001	Smith	F101	MWF9	H221	A
ART103A	S1010	Burns	F101	MWF9	H221	
ART103A	S1006	Lee	F101	MWF9	H221	B
CSC201A	S1003	Jones	F105	TUTHF10	M110	A
CSC201A	S1006	Lee	F105	TUTHF10	M110	C
HST205A	S1001	Smith	F202	MWF11	H221	

Figure 5.1 The NewClass Table

Update anomaly: If schedule of ART103A is updated in first record, and not in second and third – inconsistent data

Deletion anomaly: If record of student S1001 is deleted, information about HST205A class is lost also

Insertion anomaly: It is not possible to add a new class, for MTH101A , even if its teacher, schedule, and room are known, unless there is a student registered for it, because the key contains stuId

Normal Forms

- First normal form -1NF
- Second normal form-2NF
- Third normal form-3NF
- Boyce-Codd normal form-BCNF
- Fourth normal form-4NF
- Fifth normal form-5NF
- Domain/Key normal form-DKNF

Each is contained within the previous form – each has stricter rules than the previous form

Functional Dependency

- A **functional dependency** (FD) is a type of relationship between attributes
- If A and B are sets of attributes of relation R, say B is functionally dependent on A if each A value in R has associated with it exactly one value of B in R.
- Alternatively, if two tuples have the same A values, they must also have the same B values
- Write **A_B**, read **A functionally determines B**, or B functionally dependent on A
- FD is actually a many-to-one relationship between A and B

Example of FDs

- Let R be
NewStudent(stuId, lastName, major, credits, status, socSecNo)
- FDs in R include

{stuId}_{lastName}, but not the reverse

{stuId} _{lastName, major, credits, status, socSecNo, stuId}

{socSecNo} _{stuId, lastName, major, credits, status, socSecNo}

{credits}_{status}, but not {status}_{credits}

Trivial Functional Dependency

- The FD X_Y is **trivial** if set {Y} is a subset of set {X}

Examples: If A and B are attributes of R,
{A}_{A}
{A,B} _{A}
{A,B} _{B}
{A,B} _{A,B}
are all trivial FDs

Keys

- **Superkey** – functionally determines all attributes in a relation
- **Candidate key** - superkey that is a minimal identifier (no extraneous attributes)
- **Primary key** - candidate key actually used
- Primary key has **no-null** constraint and **uniqueness** constraint
- Should also enforce uniqueness and no-null rule for candidate keys

First Normal Form

- A relation is in **1NF** iff every attribute is single-valued for each tuple
- Each cell of the table has only one value in it
- Domains of attributes are **atomic**: no sets, lists, repeating fields or groups allowed in domains

Counter-Example for 1NF

stuId	lastName	major	credits	status	socSecNo
S1001	Smith	History	90	Senior	100429500
S1003	Jones	Math	95	Senior	010124567
S1006	Lee	CSC Math	15	Fresh	088520876
S1010	Burns	Art English	63	Junior	099320985
S1060	Jones	CSC	25	Fresh	064624738

Figure 5.4(a) NewStu Table (Assume students can have double majors)

The *major* attribute is not single-valued for each tuple

Ensuring 1NF

- Best solution: For each multi-valued attribute, create a new table, in which you place the key of the original table and the multi-valued attribute. Keep the original table, with its key

Ex. NewStu2(stuId, lastName, credits, status, socSecNo)
    Majors(stuId, major)

Another method for 1NF

- "Flatten" the original table by making the multi-valued attribute part of the key

stuId	lastName	major	credits	status	socSecNo
S1001	Smith	History	90	Senior	100429500
S1003	Jones	Math	95	Senior	010124567
S1006	Lee	CSC	15	Fresh	088520876
S1006	Lee	Math	15	Fresh	088520876
S1010	Burns	Art	63	Junior	099320985
S1010	Burns	Engllish	63	Junior	099320985
S1060	Jones	CSC	25	Fresh	064624738

Student(stuId, lastName, major, credits, status, socSecNo)

Yet Another Method

- **If the number of repeats is limited, make additional columns for multiple values**

stuId	lastName	major1	major2	credits	status	socSecNo
S1001	Smith	History		90	Senior	100429500
S1003	Jones	Math		95	Senior	010124567
S1006	Lee	CSC	Math	15	Fresh	088520876
S1010	Burns	Art	English	63	Junior	099320985
S1060	Jones	CSC		25	Fresh	064624738

Student(stuId, lastName, major1, major2, credits, status, socSecNo)

Full Functional Dependency

- In relation R, set of attributes B is **fully functionally dependent** on set of attributes A of R if B is functionally dependent on A but not functionally dependent on any proper subset of A
- This means every attribute in A is needed to functionally determine B

Notes

Partial Functional Dependency Example

NewClass(courseNo, stuId, stuLastName, facId, schedule, room, grade)

FDs:
{courseNo,stuId} _ {lastName}
{courseNo,stuId} _{facId}
{courseNo,stuId} _{schedule}
{courseNo,stuId} _{room}
{courseNo,stuId} _{grade}
courseNo _ facId   **partial FD
courseNo _ schedule **partial FD
courseNo _room ** partial FD
stuId _ lastName ** partial FD
...plus trivial FDs that are partial...

Second Normal Form

- A relation is in **second normal form** (2NF) iff it is in first normal form and all the nonkey attributes are **fully** functionally dependent on the key.
- No non-key attribute is FD on just part of the key
- If key has only one attribute, and R is 1NF, R is automatically 2NF

Converting to 2NF

- Identify each partial FD
- Remove the attributes that depend on each of the determinants so identified
- Place these determinants in separate relations along with their dependent attributes
- In original relation keep the composite key and any attributes that are fully functionally dependent on all of it
- Even if the composite key has no dependent attributes, keep that relation to connect logically the others

2NF Example

NewClass(courseNo, stuId, stuLastName, facId, schedule, room, grade)

FDs grouped by determinant:
{courseNo} _ {courseNo,facId, schedule, room}
{stuId} _ {stuId, lastName}
{courseNo,stuId} _ {courseNo, stuId, facId, schedule,
room, lastName, grade}

Create tables grouped by determinants:
Course(courseNo,facId, schedule, room)
Stu(stuId, lastName)
Keep relation with original composite key, with attributes FD on it, if any
NewStu2(courseNo, stuId, grade)

Transitive Dependency

- If A, B, and C are attributes of relation R, such that A _ B, and B _ C, then C is **transitively dependent** on A

Example:
NewStudent (stuId, lastName, major, credits, status)
FD:
credits_status

By transitivity:
stuId_credits Ÿ credits_status implies stuId_status

Transitive dependencies cause update, insertion, deletion anomalies.

Third Normal Form

- A relation is in **third normal form** (3NF) if whenever a non-trivial functional dependency X_A exists, then either X is a superkey or A is a member of some candidate key
- To be 3NF, relation must be 2NF and have no transitive dependencies
- No non-key attribute determines another non-key attribute. Here key includes "candidate key"

Making a relation 3NF

- For example,
NewStudent (stuId, lastName, major, credits, status)
with FD credits_status

- Remove the dependent attribute, *status*, from the relation
- Create a new table with the dependent attribute and its determinant, *credits*
- Keep the determinant in the original table

NewStu2 (stuId, lastName, major, credits)
Stats (credits, status)

Boyce-Codd Normal Form

- A relation is in Boyce/Codd Normal Form (BCNF) if whenever a non-trivial functional dependency X_A exists, then X is a superkey
- Stricter than 3NF, which allows A to be part of a candidate key
- If there is just one single candidate key, the forms are equivalent

Example

NewFac (facName, dept, office, rank, dateHired)

FDs:
office _ dept
facName,dept _ office, rank, dateHired
facName,office _ dept, rank, dateHired

- NewFac is not BCNF because office is not a superkey
- To make it BCNF, remove the dependent attributes to a new relation, with the determinant as the key
- Project into
Fac1 (office, dept)
Fac2 (facName, office, rank, dateHired)

Note we have lost a functional dependency in Fac2 – no longer able to see that {facName, dept} is a determinant, since they are in different relations

Properties of Decompositions

- Starting with a universal relation that contains all the attributes, we can decompose into relations by projection
- A **decomposition** of a relation R is a set of relations $\{R_1, R_2, \ldots, R_n\}$ such that each R_i is a subset of R and the union of all of the R_i is R.
- Desirable properties of decompositions
  - **Attribute preservation** - every attribute is in some relation
  - **Dependency preservation** - see previous example
  - **Lossless decomposition** - discussed later

Dependency Preservation

- If R is decomposed into $\{R_1, R_2, \ldots, R_n\}$ so that for each functional dependency X_Y all the attributes in X » Y appear in the same relation, R_i, then all FDs are preserved
- Allows DBMS to check each FD constraint by checking just one table for each

Multivalued Dependency

- In R(A,B,C) if each A values has associated with it a set of B values and a set of C values such that the B and C values are independent of each other, then **A multidetermines B** and **A multidetermines C**
- Multivalued dependencies occur in pairs
- Example: JointAppoint(facId, dept, committee) assuming a faculty member can belong to more than one department and belong to more than one committee
- Table must list all combinations of values of department and committee for each facId

4NF

- A table is **4NF** iff it is BCNF and has **no multi-valued dependencies**
- Example: remove MVDs in JointAppoint

Appoint1(facId,dept)

Appoint2(facId,committee)

Example of Lossy Projection

Original EmpRoleProj table:

EmpName	role	projName
Smith	designer	Nile
Smith	programmer	Amazon
Smith	designer	Amazon
Jones	designer	Amazon

Project into

Table a

EmpName	role
Smith	designer
Smith	programmer
Jones	designer

Table b

role	projName
designer	Nile
programmer	Amazon
designer	Amazon

Joining Table a and Table b produces

EmpName	role	projName	
Smith	designer	Nile	
Smith	designer	Amazon	
Smith	programmer	Amazon	
Jones	designer	Nile	fl spurious tuple
Jones	designer	Amazon	

Lossless Decomposition

- A decomposition of R into $\{R_1, R_2, ..., R_n\}$ is **lossless** if the natural join of $R_1, R_2,...,R_n$ produces exactly the relation R
- No **spurious tuples** are created when the projections are joined.
- always possible to find a BCNF decomposition that is lossless

Lossless Projections

- Lossless property guaranteed if for each pair of relations that will be joined, the set of common attributes is a superkey of one of the relations
- Binary decomposition of R into $\{R_1, R_2\}$ lossless iff one of these holds

  R1 _ R2 _ R1 - R2
  or
  R1 _ R2 _ R2 - R1
- For n relations in decomposition, test by general *Algorithm to Test for Lossless Join*, found on p 252
- If projection is done by successive binary projections, can apply binary decomposition test repeatedly

5NF and DKNF

- A relation is **5NF** if there are no remaining non-trivial lossless projections
- A relation is in **Domain-Key Normal Form** (DKNF) is every constraint is a logical consequence of domain constraints or key constraints

Denormalization

- When to stop the normalization process
  - When applications require too many joins
  - When you cannot get a nonloss decomposition that preserves dependencies

Inference Rules for FDs

- Armstrong's Axioms
  - **Reflexivity** If B is a subset of A, then A _ B..
  - **Augmentation** If A _ B, then AC _ BC.
  - **Transitivity** If A _ B and B _ C, then A _ C

Additional rules that follow:
  - **Additivity** If A _ B and A _ C, then A _ BC
  - **Projectivity** If A _ BC, then A _ B and A _ C
  - **Pseudotransitivity** If A _ B and CB _ D, then AC _ D

Closure of Set of FDs

- If F is a set of functional dependencies for a relation R, then the set of all functional dependencies that can be derived from F, F^+, is called the **closure of F**

- Could compute closure by applying Armstrong's Axioms repeatedly

Closure of an Attribute

- If A is an attribute or set of attributes of relation R, all the attributes in R that are functionally dependent on A in R form the **closure of A**, A^+

- Computed by Closure Algorithm for A, p 256
  result _ A;
  while (result changes) do
  * for each functional dependency B _ C in F*
  *   if B is contained in result then result _ result » C;*
  end;
  A^+ _ result;

Uses of Attribute Closure

- Can determine if A is a superkey-if every attribute in R functionally dependent on A
- Can determine whether a given FD X_Y is in the closure of the set of FDs. (Find X^+, see if it includes Y)

Redundant FDs and Covers

- Given a set of FDs, can determine if any of them is **redundant**, i.e. can be derived from the remaining FDs, by a simple algorithm – see p 257
- If a relation R has two sets of FDs, F and G
  - then F is a **cover** for G if every FD in G is also in F^+
  - F and G are equivalent if F is a cover for G and G is a cover for F (i.e. $F^+ = G^+$)

Minimal Set of FDs

- Set of FDs, F is **minimal** if
  - The right side of every FD in F has a single attribute (called standard or canonical form)
  - No attribute in the left side of any FD is extraneous
  - F has no redundant FDs

Minimal Cover for Set of FDs

- A minimal cover for a set of FDs is a cover such that no proper subset of itself is also a cover
- A set of FDs may have several minimal covers
- See *Algorithm for Finding a Minimal Cover*, p 259

Decomposition Algorithm for BCNF

- Can always find a lossless decomposition that is BCNF
  - Find a FD that is a violation of BCNF and remove it by decomposition process
  - Repeat this process until all violations are removed
  - See algorithm, p 260
- No need to go through 1NF, 2NF, 3NF process
- Not always possible to preserve all FDs

Synthesis Algorithm for 3NF

- Can always find 3NF decomposition that is lossless **and that preserves all FDs**
- 3NF Algorithm uses synthesis
  - Begin with universal relation and set of FDs,G
  - Find a minimal cover for G
  - Combine FDs that have the same determinant
  - Include a relation with a key of R
  - See algorithm p 260

Notes

Databases Illuminated

Databases Illuminated
Catherine Ricardo

Databases Illuminated

Chapter 6
**Relational Database
Management Systems and SQL**

History of SQL

- Proposed by E.F.Codd in his 1970 paper
- Used in System R, IBM's research relational database in early 1970s-D.D. Chamberlin et al at IBM Research Center, San Jose, California
- Used in Oracle, released in late 1970s
- Incorporated into IBM's SQL/DS in 1981, and DB2 in 1983
- Also used in Microsoft SQL Server, MySQL, Informix, Sybase, dBase, Paradox, r:Base, FoxPro, and others

---

Standards

- ANSI and ISO published SQL standards in 1986, called SQL-1
- Minor revision, SQL-89
- Major revision, SQL-2,1992
- SQL-3, multi-part revision, contains SQL:1999, which included object-oriented (OO) facilities, and user defined datatypes (UDTs)
- Most vendors support standard, but have slight variations of their own

---

Components of SQL

- Data definition language - DDL
- Data manipulation language - DML
- Authorization language – grant privileges to users

Relational Database Architecture

- Separate external, logical, internal models
- Base tables and indexes form logical level
- Indexes are B+ trees or B trees – maintained by system
- Relational views (external level) are derived from base tables
- Users see views or base tables, or combination
- Internal level - files
- SQL supports dynamic database definition-can modify structures easily
- See Figure 6.1

DDL Commands

CREATE TABLE
CREATE INDEX
ALTER TABLE
RENAME TABLE
DROP TABLE
DROP INDEX
Also – CREATE VIEW

CREATE TABLE

CREATE TABLE *base-table-name* (*colname datatype*
[*column constraints* – NULL/NOT NULL, DEFAULT...,
UNIQUE, CHECK..., PRIMARY KEY],
[,*colname datetype* [*column constraints* ...]]
...
[*table constraints* – PRIMARY KEY..., FOREIGN KEY...,
UNIQUE..., CHECK...]
[*storage specifications*]);

Identifiers

- No SQL keywords may be used
- Table name must be unique within the database
- For each column, the user must specify a name that is unique within the table

Datatypes

- Each column must have a datatype specified
- Standards include various numeric types, fixed-length and varying-length character strings, bit strings, and user-defined types
- available data types vary from DBMS to DBMS
- Oracle types include CHAR(N), VARCHAR2(N), NUMBER(N,D), DATE, and BLOB (binary large object) and others
- DB2 types include SMALLINT, INTEGER, BIGINT, DECIMAL/NUMERIC, REAL, DOUBLE, CHAR(N), VARCHAR(N), LONG VARCHAR, CLOB, GRAPHIC, DBCLOB, BLOB, DATE, TIME, and TIMESTAMP
- SQL Server includes types of NUMERIC, BINARY, CHAR, VARCHAR DATETIME, MONEY, IMAGE, and others
- Access supports several types of NUMBER, as well as TEXT, MEMO, DATE/TIME, CURRENCY, YES/NO, and others

Creating the Tables for the University Database

```
CREATE TABLE Student          (
    stuId                     CHAR(6),
    lastName                  CHAR(20)  NOT NULL,
    firstName                 CHAR(20)  NOT NULL,
    major                     CHAR(10),
    credits                   SMALLINT DEFAULT 0,
    CONSTRAINT Student_stuId_pk PRIMARY KEY (stuId),
    CONSTRAINT Student_credits_cc CHECK (credits>=0 AND credits < 150));
CREATE TABLE Faculty          (
    facId                     CHAR(6),
    name                      CHAR(20)  NOT NULL,
    department                CHAR(20)  NOT NULL,
    rank                      CHAR(10),
    CONSTRAINT Faculty_facId_pk PRIMARY KEY (facId));
CREATE TABLE Class            (
    classNumber               CHAR(8),
    facId                     CHAR(6)  NOT NULL,
    schedule                  CHAR(8),
    room                      CHAR(6),
    CONSTRAINT Class_classNumber_pk PRIMARY KEY (classNumber),
    CONSTRAINT Class_facId_fk FOREIGN KEY (facId) REFERENCES Faculty (facId));
CREATE TABLE Enroll           (
    stuId                     CHAR(6),
    classNumber               CHAR(8),
    grade                     CHAR(2),
    CONSTRAINT Enroll_classNumber_stuId_pk PRIMARY KEY (classNumber, stuId),
    CONSTRAINT Enroll_classNumber_fk FOREIGN KEY (classNumber) REFERENCES Class (classNumber),
    CONSTRAINT Enroll_stuId_fk FOREIGN KEY (stuId) REFERENCES Student(stuId));
```

New Datatypes

- SQL:1999 provides new UDTs
- Can define structured UDTs
- Also new DISTINCT types e.g.
  ```
  CREATE DOMAIN creditValues INTEGER
  DEFAULT 0
  CHECK (VALUE >=0 AND VALUE <150);
  ```
- New type can then be used in defining columns
  In Student, can write credits creditValues,...
- Can't compare values of two different DISTINCT types, even if underlying datatype is the same
- Also can't apply functions to them, but can write our own functions for them

...will be discussed more fully in Chapter 7

Constraints

- Can be defined at column level or table level
- Column-level constraints
  - NULL/NOT NULL, UNIQUE, PRIMARY KEY, CHECK and DEFAULT
  - Written immediately after column name, datatype
- Table-level constraints
  - Primary key, foreign keys, uniqueness, checks, and general constraints
  - Note: any primary key can be defined at table level; composite primary keys can only be expressed as table-level constraints
  - Foreign key constraint requires that the referenced table exist already
  - SQL standard supports ON UPDATE and ON DELETE clauses for foreign keys; Options are CASCADE/SET NULL/SET DEFAULT/NO ACTION; Example: ON UPDATE CASCADE
  - Table uniqueness constraint used to specify values in a combination of columns must be unique; good for candidate keys
  - Constraints can be given a name; useful for disabling them at times
  - NOTE: Not all options are supported in all DBMSs

Indexes

- Can create any number of indexes for tables
- Stored in same file as base table
- Facilitate fast retrieval of records with specific values in a column
- Keep track of what values exist for the indexed columns, and which records have those values
- B+ trees or B trees used – see Appendix A for review of concepts
- Overhead – system must maintain index

CREATE INDEX Command

CREATE [UNIQUE] INDEX *indexname* **ON** *basetablename* (*colname* [*order*] [,*colname* [*order*]]...) **[CLUSTER]** ;

Ex. CREATE INDEX Student_lastName_firstName_ndx ON Student (lastName, firstName);
- UNIQUE specification enforces unique values for indexed column or combination of columns
- Except when specified, column need not be unique
- Order is ASC(default) or DESC
- Can have major and minor orders
- CLUSTER specification keeps records with same value for indexed field together (only one per table)
- Oracle automatically indexes primary key columns

ALTER TABLE Command

- To add a new column

ALTER TABLE *basetablename* ADD *columnname datatype*;
Ex. ALTER TABLE Student ADD COLUMN birthdate DATETYPE;
  - Cannot specify NOT NULL, since existing records have no value for this field

- To drop a column

ALTER TABLE *basetablename* DROP COLUMN *columnname*;
Ex. ALTER TABLE Student DROP COLUMN major;

- To add a constraint

ALTER TABLE *basetablename* ADD CONSTRAINT *constraint_defn*;

- To drop a constraint

ALTER TABLE *basetablename* DROP CONSTRAINT *constraint_name*;

Other Changes to Tables

- Renaming a table:

RENAME TABLE *old-table-name* **TO** *new-table-name;*
Ex: RENAME TABLE FACULTY TO TEACHERS;

- Dropping a table:

DROP TABLE *basetablename;*
Ex. DROP TABLE CLASS;

- Dropping an index:

DROP INDEX *indexname;*
Ex. DROP INDEX Student_lastName_fristName_ndx;

SQL DML

- Non-procedural, declarative language
- Can be interactive, can be embedded in host language, or can be stand-alone programming language (SQL/PSMs)
- Basic commands
    - SELECT
    - UPDATE
    - INSERT
    - DELETE

SELECT Statement

SELECT	[DISTINCT] *col-name* [AS *newname*], [,*col-name*..]…
FROM	*table-name* [*alias*] [,*table-name*]…
[**WHERE**	*predicate*]
[GROUP BY	*col-name* [,*col-name*]…[HAVING *predicate*]
or	
[ORDER BY	*col-name* [,*col-name*]…];

- Powerful command – equivalent to relational algebra's SELECT, PROJECT, JOIN and more…
- Can be applied to one or more tables or views
- Can display one or more columns (renaming if desired)
- Predicate is optional, and may include usual operators and connectives
- Can put results in order by one or more columns
- Can also group together records with the same value for column(s)
- Can also use predefined functions
- See list of examples, Section 6.4

UPDATE Operator

UPDATE   *tablename*
SET   *columnname = expression*
              [*columnname = expression*]...
[WHERE *predicate*];

- Used for changing values in existing records
- Can update, zero, one, many, or all records in a table
- For null value, use SET *columnname = NULL*
- can use a subquery to identify records to be updated

INSERT Operator

INSERT
INTO   *tablename* [(*colname* [,*colname*]...)]
VALUES (*constant* [,*constant*]...);

- Used for inserting new records into database, one at a time
- Not necessary to name columns if values are supplied for all columns, in proper order
- To insert null value for a column, specify only the other columns or write *null* as the value
- Can specify values for some columns, in any order, as long as values match order

DELETE Operator

DELETE
FROM   *tablename*
WHERE   *predicate*;
- Used for deleting existing records from database
- Can delete zero, one, many, or all records
- Operation may not work if referential integrity would be lost
- Can use a subquery to target records to be deleted
- If you delete all records from a table, its structure still remains, and you can insert into it later

Relational Views

- Can be subsets of base tables, or subsets of joins, or contain calculated data
- Reasons for views
  - Allow different users to see the data in different forms
  - Provide a simple authorization control device
  - Free users from complicated DML operations
  - If database is restructured, view can keep the user's model constant

Create View

```
CREATE VIEW viewname [(viewcolname
    [,viewcolname]...)] AS      SELECT     colname
    [,colname]...
    FROM       basetablename [,basetablename]...
    WHERE      condition;
```

- Can create vertical subset of table, choosing only certain columns, with no WHERE, called **value-independent** view
- Can choose only certain rows, using WHERE, called **value-dependent** view
- Can use a join of tables to create view of combination
- Can use functions in SELECT

Using Views

- Can write new SQL statements using view name in FROM line
- Can create a view of a view
- Can sometimes update a view – requires that the primary key be in the view
- When user is allowed to update using view, DB administrator can provide an INSTEAD OF trigger to update base tables instead

```
CREATE TRIGGER InsertStuVw2
INSTEAD OF INSERT ON StudentVw2
FOR EACH ROW
begin
    INSERT
    INTO    Student
    VALUES (:NEW.stuId, :NEW.lastName, :NEW.firstName, :NEW. Credits);
end;
```

Notes

Active Databases-Constraints

- DBMS monitors database to prevent illegal states, using constraints and triggers
- Constraints
  - can be specified when table is created, or later
  - IMMEDIATE MODE: constraint checked when each INSERT, DELETE, UPDATE is performed
  - DEFERRED MODE: postpones constraint checking to end of transaction – write SET CONSTRAINT *name* DEFERRED
  - Can use DISABLE CONSTRAINT *name*, and later ENABLE CONSTRAINT *name*

Triggers

- More flexible than constraints
- Must have ECA model:
  - **event**, some change made to the database
  - **condition**, a logical predicate
  - **action**, a procedure done when the event occurs and the condition is true, also called **firing the trigger**
- Can be fired before or after insert, update, delete
- Trigger can access values it needs as :OLD. and :NEW.
  - prefix :OLD refers to values in a tuple deleted or to the values replaced in an update
  - prefix :NEW refers to the values in a tuple just inserted or to the new values in an update.
- Can specify whether trigger fires just once for each triggering statement, or for each row that is changed by the statement

Trigger Syntax

CREATE OR REPLACE TRIGGER *trigger_name*
[BEFORE/AFTER] [INSERT/UPDATE/DELETE] ON
  table_name
[FOR EACH ROW] [WHEN *condition*]
BEGIN
  trigger body
END;

- Can disable triggers using ALTER TRIGGER *name* DISABLE;
- Later write ALTER TRIGGER *name* ENABLE;
- Can drop triggers using DROP TRIGGER *name*;
- See examples in Figure 6.5

Ending Transactions

- COMMIT makes permanent changes in the current transaction
- ROLLBACK undoes changes made by the current transaction

SQL Programming

- SQL can be embedded in host languages, such as Java, C++, COBOL, and so on
- Host language can provide control structures, and SQL used for database access
- Executable SQL statements preceded by keyword such as EXEC SQL, end with ;
- Executable SQL statement can appear wherever a host language executable statement can appear
- Precompiler for DB compiles SQL separately from program; creates access module
- Host language statements compiled as usual
- Data exchange done using shared variables

Shared Variables

- Declared in SQL declaration section. Ex:
  ```
  EXEC SQL BEGIN DECLARE SECTION;
  char stuNumber[5];
  char stuLastName[15];
  char stuFirstName[12];
  char stuMajor[10];
  int stuCredits;
  char SQLSTATE[6];
  EXEC SQL END DECLARE SECTION;
  ```
- **SQLSTATE** used for error conditions—'00000' means no error, while '02000' means no tuple found for query
- Value of SQLSTATE should be tested in host language control statements such as WHILE(SQLSTATE='00000') or UNTIL(SQLSTATE='02000')

Notes

Single-row Embedded SQL SELECT

```
stuNumber = 'S1001';
EXEC SQL     SELECT Student.lastName, Student.firstName,
        Student.major, Student.credits
        INTO    :stuLastName, :stuFirstName, :stuMajor, :stuCredits
        FROM   Student
        WHERE Student.stuId = :stuNumber;
```

- INTO line lists shared variables declared previously
- In SQL statements, use colon before shared variables to distinguish them from database attributes; they may have the same or different names from attributes
- In the host language, use the shared variables without colon, ex

`if(stuCredits>120)...`

Insert in Embedded SQL

- Assign values to program shared variables
- Use SQL INSERT, listing shared variables (now preceded by colon) as values

Ex:

```
stuNumber = 'S1050';
stuLastName = 'Lee';
stuFirstName = 'Daphne';
stuMajor = 'English';
stuCredits = 0;
EXEC SQL   INSERT
        INTO Student (stuId, lastName, firstName, major, credits)
        VALUES(:stuNumber,:stuLastName,:stuFirstName,:stuMajor,
            :stuCredits);
```

Delete in Embedded SQL

- Use program shared variables to identify target tuple(s)
- Use SQL DELETE, identifying tuple(s) in WHERE line using shared variables (preceded by colon)

Ex:

```
stuNumber = 'S1015';
EXEC SQL     DELETE
        FROM        Student
        WHERE stuId = :stuNumber;
```

Update in Embedded SQL

- Use program shared variables to identify target tuple(s)
- Use SQL UPDATE, identifying tuple(s) in WHERE line using shared variables preceded by colon

```
Ex:
stuMajor = 'History';
EXEC SQL          UPDATE Student
                  SET     CREDITS = CREDITS + 3
                  WHERE major = :stuMajor;
```

Error Handling using WHENEVER

- Can check each SQL transaction individually, or do error-handling for entire program using WHENEVER
- SQLERROR means any exception
- NOT FOUND means SQLSTATE of '02000'

EXEC SQL WHENEVER [SQLERROR/NOT FOUND][CONTINUE/ GO TO *statement*];

Using Cursors

- Impedence mismatch: SQL SELECT can retrieve multiple rows, while host language requires one row at a time
- Cursor can be created and positioned to provide one tuple at a time to program
- Declaring a cursor:
  ```
  EXEC SQL DECLARE cursorname [INSENSITIVE] [SCROLL] CURSOR FOR query
  [FOR {READ ONLY | UPDATE OF attributeNames}];
  ```
- Query is regular SQL query, using attributes names (not the shared variables)
- Opening the cursor executes the SQL query
  ```
  EXEC SQL OPEN cursorname;
  ```
- Set up a loop in host language
  ```
  WHILE (SQLSTATE = '00000')
  ```
- To retrieve each row of the results, use FETCH
  ```
  EXEC SQL FETCH cursorname INTO hostvariables;
  ```
- *hostvariables* are shared variables; preceded by colon
- At end, close the cursor
  ```
  EXEC SQL CLOSE cursorname;
  ```

Cursor Example

```
EXEC SQL DECLARE CSCstuCursor CURSOR FOR
    SELECT stuId, lastName, firstName, major, credits
    FROM student
    WHERE major='CSC';
EXEC SQL OPEN CSCstuCursor;
WHILE (SQLSTATE = '00000')
    EXEC SQL FETCH CSCstuCursor INTO
        :stuNumber,:stuLastName, :stuFirstName,:stuMajor,:stuCredits
        //Process each record retrieved
END; //of WHILE
EXEC SQL CLOSE CSCstuCursor;
```

Update and Delete Using a Cursor

- Must declare cursor for update: FOR UPDATE OF *variablename*
- Once cursor is open and active, current of cursor refers to the tuple it is positioned at
- To update:
  ```
  EXEC SQL UPDATE tablename
  SET attributename = newvalue
  WHERE CURRENT OF cursorname;
  ```
- To delete:
  ```
  EXEC SQL DELETE FROM tablename
  WHERE CURRENT OF cursorname;
  ```

Update and Delete Examples

```
EXEC SQL DECLARE stuCreditsCursor CURSOR FOR
    SELECT stuId, credits
    FROM Student
    FOR UPDATE OF credits;
EXEC SQL OPEN stuCreditsCursor;
WHILE (SQLSTATE = '00000')
    EXEC SQL FETCH stuCreditsCursor INTO :stuNumber, ::stuCredits
    EXEC SQL    UPDATE Student
                SET credits = credits +3
                WHERE CURRENT OF stuCreditsCursor;
END; //of WHILE loop
```

- For delete, replace update statement by
  ```
  EXEC SQL    DELETE FROM Student
              WHERE CURRENT OF stuCreditCursor;
  ```
- Could target specific tuples in the SQL SELECT statement for declaration of cursor

Dynamic SQL

- Can create a graphical front end that accepts queries dynamically
- At run time, user prompted to enter an SQL command
- Command stored as string
- PREPARE statement used to parse and compile string and assign it to variable
- EXECUTE command executes the code
- Ex

```
char userString[ ]='UPDATE Student SET credits = 36
    WHERE stuId= S1050';
EXEC SQL PREPARE userCommand FROM :userString;
EXEC SQL EXECUTE userCommand;
```

API, ODBC and JDBC

- DBMS can provide a library of functions available to host languages using an API
- ODBC/JDBC provide standardized connectivity using a common interface, allows common code to access different databases
- Most vendors provide ODBC or JDBC drivers that conform to the standard
- Requires four components: application, driver manager, driver, and data source (database)

ODBC/JDBC Components

- **Application,** using the standard API
  - initiates the connection with the database
  - submits data requests as SQL statements to the DBMS
  - retrieves the results
  - performs processing
  - terminates the connection
- **Driver manager**
  - loads and unloads drivers at the application's request
  - passes the ODBC or JDBC calls to the selected driver
- **Database driver**
  - links the application to the data source
  - translates the ODBC or JDBC calls to DBMS-specific calls
  - handles data translation needed because of any differences between the DBMS's data language and the ODBC/JDBC standard
  - Controls error handling differences that arise between the data source and the standard.
- **Data source**: database (or other source), DBMS and platform; provides the data

Notes

SQL/PSM

- Persistent Stored Modules-used to create internal routines within database space
- Can be saved with database schema and invoked
- Oracle uses PL/SQL, accessed within SQLPlus
- Provides complete programming language facilities-declarations, control, assignment, functions, procedures, temporary relations, etc.

SQL/PSM Procedures and Functions

- Creating procedures
  CREATE PROCEDURE *procedure_name* (*parameter_list*)
      declarations of local variables
      procedure code
  - Parameters may be IN, OUT, or IN/OUT
  - Executing procedures-Example:
  EXECUTE *procedure_name(actual_ parameter_ list)*;
- Creating functions
  CREATE FUNCTION *function_name* (*parameter list*) RETURNS
      SQLdatatype
      declarations of local variables
      function code (must include a RETURN statement)
  - Parameters can be IN only, no OUT or IN/OUT
  - A function is invoked by using its name, typically in an assignment statement..Example:
      SET newVal = MyFunction(val1, val2);

Declaration, Assignment, Control Statements in SQL/PSM

- DECLARE *identifier datatype*;

- SET number_of_courses = credits/3;

- IF (*condition*) THEN *statements*;
  ELSEIF (*condition*) *statements*;
  ...
      ELSEIF (*condition*) *statements*;
      ELSE *statements*;
  END IF;

- CASE *selector*
      WHEN *value1*   THEN *statements*;
      WHEN *value2*   THEN *statements*;
  ...
  END CASE;

- LOOP...ENDLOOP, WHILE... DO... END WHILE, REPEAT...UNTIL...END REPEAT, and FOR ...DO... END FOR

System Catalog

- Also called system data dictionary
- Contains metadata
- Automatically updated when new database objects created – stores schema
- Oracle data dictionary provides three views: USER, ALL, and DBA.
- View invoked by using the appropriate term as a prefix for the object(s) named in the FROM clause in a query
  - **USER view** provides a user with information about all the objects created by that user
  - **ALL view** provides information about objects user has permission to access in addition to the one the user has created.
  - **DBA view** provides information about all database objects; available to the database administrator

Using Oracle Data Dictionary-Examples

```
DESCRIBE STUDENT;
DESCRIBE USER_CONSTRAINTS;

SELECT CONSTRAINT_NAME, CONSTRAINT_TYPE, TABLE_NAME
FROM USER_CONSTRAINTS;

SELECT TABLE_NAME
FROM USER_TABLES;

SELECT VIEW_NAME
FROM USER_VIEWS;

SELECT TRIGGER_NAME, TRIGGER_EVENT, TRIGGER_TYPE
FROM USER_TRIGGERS;

SELECT *
FROM USER_TAB_COLUMNS;

SELECT COLUMN_NAME, DATA_TYPE
FROM USER_TAB_COLUMNS
WHERE TABLE_NAME = 'STUDENT';
```

IBM DB2 UDB Catalog

- system catalog in a schema called SYSIBM, usually with restricted access
- Two views, SYSCAT and SYSSTAT, are available for users
- **SYSCAT schema:**
  - TABLES(TABSCHEMA, TABNAME, DEFINER, TYPE, STATUS, COLCOUNT, KEYCOLUMNS, CHECKCOUNT, ...)
  - COLUMNS(TABSCHEMA, TABNAME, COLNAME, COLNO, TYPENAME, LENGTH, DEFAULT, NULLS, ...)
  - INDEXES(INDSCHEMA, INDNAME, DEFINER, TABSCHEMA, TABNAME, COLNAMES, UNIQUERULE, COLCOUNT, ...)
  - TRIGGERS(TRIGSCHEMA, TRIGNAME, DEFINER, TABSCHEMA, TABNAME, TRIGTIME, TRIGEVENT, ...)
  - VIEWS(VIEWSCHEMA, VIEWNAME, DEFINER, TEXT,...)
- Can query this database using usual SQL SELECT statements
  ```
  SELECT TABLESCHEMA, TABLENAME
  FROM TABLES
  WHERE DEFINER = 'JONES';

  SELECT *
  FROM COLUMNS
  WHERE TABNAME = 'STUDENT'
  GROUP BY COLNAME;
  ```

Chapter 7: The Enhanced Entity Relationship Model and Object-Relational Model

Notes

Databases Illuminated
Catherine Ricardo

Databases Illuminated

Chapter 7
The Enhanced Entity-Relationship
Model and the Object-Relational
Model

Why Extend the E-R Model?

- E-R suitable for traditional business applications
- E-R not semantically rich enough for advanced applications
- Applications where E-R is inadequate
  - Geographical information systems
  - Search engines
  - Data mining
  - Multimedia
  - CAD/CAM
  - Software development
  - Engineering design...and others

Specialization Abstraction

- Specialization-needed when an entity set has subsets that have special attributes or that participate in special relationships
- Process of breaking up a class into subclasses
  Ex: Faculty contains AdjunctFac and FullTimeFac
  - All Faculty have attributes facid, lastName, firstName, rank.
  - AdjunctFac also have coursePayRate
  - FullTimeFac have annualSalary

Representing Specialization

- E-ER diagram – See Figure 7.1(a) - shows specialization circle (*isa* relationship), and inheritance symbol (subset symbol)
- Specialization can also involve just one subclass – no need for circle, but show inheritance symbol –see Figure 7.1(b)
  Ex. Class has LabClass specialization
- Subclasses can participate in their own relationships – See Figure 7.1(c)
  Ex. FullTimeFac *subscribes to* Pension

Generalization Abstraction

- Inverse of specialization
- Recognizing that classes have common properties and identifying a superclass for them
  Ex. Student and Faculty are both people
- Bottom-up process, as opposed to top-down process of specialization
- EER diagram is the same as for specialization – See Figure 7.1(d)

Generalization/Specialization Constraints

- **Subclasses can be overlapping or disjoint**
- Place **o** or **d** in specialization circle to indicate constraint
- Specialization can be **total** (every member of superclass must be in some subclass) or **partial**
  - Total -double line connecting superclass to specialization circle
  - Partial-single line
- Specialization definition can be
  - **predicate-defined** - each subclass has a defining predicate
  - **Attribute defined** – the value of the **same** attribute is used in defining predicate for all subclasses
  - **User-defined** – user responsible for identifying proper subclass

Multiple Specializations

- Can have different specializations for the same class

Ex. Figure 7.3(a) shows undergraduates specialized by year and by residence. These are independent of each other

- Can have shared subclasses – have multiple inheritance from two or more superclasses

Ex. Figure 7.3(b) shows Teaching Assistant as subclass of both Faculty and Student

Union or Category

- Subclass related to a collection of superclasses
- Each instance of subclass belongs to one, not all, of the superclasses
- Superclasses form a **union** or **category**

Ex. A Sponsor may be a team, a department, or a club – Figure 7.4(a), top portion

- Each Sponsor entity instance is a member of **one** of these superclasses, so Sponsor is a subclass of the union of Team, Dept, Club
- EER diagram - connect each superclass to union circle, connect circle to subclass, with subset symbol on line bet circle and subclass

Total and Partial Unions

- **Total category** – every member of the sets that make up the union must participate
  - Shown on E-ER by double line from union circle to subset
  - In Figure 7.4(b) every Concert or Fair must be a CampusWideEvent
- **Partial category** – not every member of the sets must participate
  - Shown by single line
  - In Figure 7.4(b) not every Club, Team, or Dept must be a Sponsor

Total Union vs Specialization

- Total union can often be replaced by hierarchy
- Choose hierarchy representation if superclasses have many common attributes
- See Figure 7.5

(min..max) Notation for Relationships

- Shows both cardinality and participation constraints
- Can be used for both E-R and E-ER diagrams
- Use pair of integers (min..max) on line connecting entity to relationship diamond
  - **min** is the least number of relationship instances an entity must participate in
  - **max** is the greatest number it can participate in (can write M or N for many); some authors use * for many
  - See Figures 7.6 and 7.7

E-ER to Relational Model -1

- For entity sets that are not part of generalization or union, do the mapping as usual
  - Map strong entity sets to tables, with column for each attribute, but
    - For composite attributes, create column for each component, or single column for composite
    - For multi-valued attribute, create separate table with primary key of entity, plus multi-valued attribute as composite key
  - Weak entity sets – include primary key of owner
  - Binary Relationships
    - 1-M: use key of "one" side as foreign key in "many" side
    - 1-1: use either key as foreign key in the other's table
    - M-M: create relationship table with both primary keys
  - Higher-Order Relationships-create relationship table

E-ER to Relational Model-2

- **Mapping Class Hierarchies to Tables**
  - **Method 1**: Create a table for superclass and one for each of the subclasses, placing primary key of superclass in each subclass
    - Ex :   Faculty(*facId*, lastName, firstName, rank)
         AdjunctFac(*facId*, coursePayRate)
         FullTimeFac(*facId*, annualSalary)
  - **Method 2**: Create table for each subclass, including all attributes of superclass in each, with no table for superclass
    - Ex: AdjunctFac(*facId*, lastName, firstName, rank, coursePayRate)
      FullTimeFac(*facId*, lastName, firstName, rank, annualSalary)
  - **Method 3**: Create a single table with all attributes of superclass and of all subclasses
    - Ex: AllFac(*facId*, lastName, firstName, rank, annualSalary, coursePayRate)
  - Variation of method 3 is to add a "type field" to each record, indicating subclass it belongs to

E-ER to Relational Model-3

- **Mapping Unions**
  - create table for the union itself, and individual tables for each of the superclasses, using foreign keys to connect them. Include a type code field in union table

Ex:

   CampusWideEvent(*eventName*, date, time, **eventType**)
   Concert(*eventName*, performer)
   Fair(*eventName*, theme, charity)

- If superclasses have different primary keys, create a surrogate key which will be the primary key of the union

Ex:

   Sponsor(**sponsorId**, sponsorType)
   Club(*clubName*, president, numberOfMembers, **sponsorId**)
   Team(*teamName*, coach, sport, **sponsorId**)
   Department(*deptName*, deptCode, office, **sponsorId**)

SQL:1999 Object-Relational Features

- Richer fundamental data types, including types for multimedia – text, images, video, audio, etc.
- Collection types that can hold multiple attributes
- User-defined data types, including user-written operations to manipulate them
- Representation of class hierarchies, with inheritance of both data structures and methods
- Reference or pointer types for objects
  - enable us to refer to large objects such as multimedia files that are stored elsewhere
  - Can also store relationships, replacing foreign keys
- **NOTE: This discussion is about standard SQL:1999. Oracle and other DBMSs have different syntax**

New Data Types

- SQL:1999 added two new fundamental data types
  - **BOOLEAN**
    Ex. To add a matriculated field to the Student table
    matriculated BOOLEAN DEFAULT false
  - **LARGE OBJECT (LOB)**
    - Store text, audio, video, multimedia objects, signatures, etc.
    - Have very restricted functions, such as substring operations
    - Comparisons only for equality or inequality.
    - Cannot be used for ordering or in GROUP BY or ORDER BY clauses
    - large files, normally simply stored and rarely retrieved again
    - Manipulated using a LOB locator, a system-generated binary surrogate for the actual value.
    - Ex: If we stored students' signatures, add in CREATE TABLE command
      signature CLOB REF IS sigid SYSTEM GENERATED,
      - sigid is a pointer to the file containing an image of the signature
    - Variants: **BLOB** (BINARY LARGE OBJECT) and **CLOB** (CHARACTER LARGE OBJECT)
- new type constructors, **ARRAY** and **ROW**

Array Type

- **ARRAY[n]**
  - Ordered collection of values of the same base data type stored as a single attribute
  - must specify the base type
    - *attribute-name basetype* ARRAY [*n*]
  - Ex: If we allow students to have double majors, specify in CREATE TABLE
    majors   VARCHAR(10) ARRAY[2],   //Oracle does not use this syntax
  - Use constructor to create array of values
    INSERT INTO Stu VALUES('S555', 'Quirk','Sean', true,
    ARRAY['French','Psychology'], 30);
  - Use standard square bracket notation to refer to individual elements
  SELECT Stu.majors[1]
  FROM Stu
  WHERE stuId = 'S999';

Declaring Row Type

- declaration of **ROW type**
  - sequence of pairs of field names and data types
  - can use the ROW type declaration to create a data type and then use the type to create a table
  - Ex:
  CREATE ROW TYPE team_row_type(
      teamName   CHAR(20),
      coach   CHAR(30),
      sport   CHAR(15));

  CREATE TABLE Team OF TYPE team_row_type;
- can refer to an individual field using the dot notation, as in
  SELECT Team.coach
  FROM Team
  WHERE Team.sport= 'soccer';

Nested Tables Using Row Type

- An attribute can have a row-type, allowing nested tables.
- Ex: An attribute of a table can represent one team the student belongs to:

```
CREATE TABLE NewStu (
    stuId   CHAR(6),
    ...
    team   team_row_type,
    ...);
```

Arrays of Row Types

- The ROW constructor can use any data type for its fields, including ROW and ARRAY.
- Ex: student's record may have an array of teams:

```
CREATE TABLE NewStu2 (
    stuId           CHAR(6),
    lastName        CHAR(20) NOT NULL,
    firstName       CHAR(20) NOT NULL,
    matriculated    BOOLEAN DEFAULT false;
    teams           team_row_type ARRAY[3],
    majors          CHAR(10) ARRAY[2],
    credits         SMALLINT DEFAULT 0,
    CONSTRAINT...);
```

Using Array and Row Constructors

- Insert NewStu2 records using ARRAY and ROW constructors

```
INSERT INTO NewStu2 VALUES('S999', 'Smith', 'Michael',
    true, ARRAY[ROW('Angels','Jones','soccer'),
    ROW('Devils','Chin','swimming'),ROW('Tigers','Walters','
    basketball')], ARRAY['Math', 'Biology'], 60);
```

Notes

Accessing Attributes within Arrays and Rows

- Can refer to the individual attributes using nested dot notation

Ex: To retrieve all coaches for teams that a student is on

```
SELECT NewStu2.teams.coach
FROM NewStu2
WHERE stuId = "S999";
```

To get only the coach of the first team, use
SELECT NewStu2.teams[1].coach FROM…

User-defined Distinct Types

- Can construct user-defined **DISTINCT data type**, from a base type
- Ex

```
CREATE DISTINCT TYPE studentAgeType AS INTEGER;
CREATE DISTINCT TYPE numberOfCreditsType AS INTEGER;
```

- cannot compare a studentAgeType attribute with a numberofCreditsType attribute.

User-defined Structured Types

- **User-defined structured data types (UDTs)** can have several attributes
- Attributes can be any SQL type, including built-in types, LOB types, ARRAY or ROW types, or other structured types
- Can nest structured types
- a structured UDT can be either the type used for an attribute, or the type used for a table
- Attributes can be stored items or they can be virtual
- Type can be **instantiable**, which allows instances of the type to be created, or **not instantiable**
- SQL provides a default **constructor function** for instantiable types
  - Has the same name and data type as the UDT
  - Invoke it by using the name of the type
  - Takes no parameters; assigns default values to the instance attributes
- Users can also create their own constructors

Notes

Operations on UDTs

- UDTs have only a few basic operations predefined on them
  - Default constructor
  - Automatic **observer** methods that return the values of attributes
  - Automatic **mutator** methods that allow values to be assigned to attributes
  - User can override these methods by redefining them, but they cannot be overloaded
- Built-in functions (SUM, COUNT, MAX, MIN,AVG) are **not** defined for these types
- Users define operations on their UDTs by building on the basic operations defined for the source types
- The definition of a new type includes a list of its **attributes** and its **methods**
- Methods are defined only for a single user-defined type, and do not apply to other types the user creates
- Structured types can be manipulated using operations defined by the user as methods, functions, and procedures

Example of UDT

- We define a new StudentType as follows:
```
CREATE TYPE StudentType AS
(stuld       VARCHAR(6),
lastName     VARCHAR(15),
firstName    VARCHAR(12),
advisorId    VARCHAR2(6),
credits      SMALLINT,
dateOfBirth  DATE)
METHOD    addCredits(smallint);
INSTANTIABLE
NOT FINAL
```

Type Definition Components

- Type definition contains
  - The name of the type
  - List of attributes with their data types within parentheses
    - Attributes can be previously-defined UDTs
  - List of methods (if any) for the type
    - Indicate the argument types and return type (if any) for each method
  - Note that we do not indicate a primary key for the type, since we are defining a type, not a table

Writing and Using Methods

- The code for the methods is written separately
- Within the method, the implicit parameter is referred to as *self*
- Ex: The code for the addCredits method might be

```
CREATE METHOD addCredits (numberOfCredits smallint) FOR StudentType
BEGIN
      SET self.credits = self.credits + numberOfCredits;
END;
```

- When invoked, a method takes an instance of the type as an implicit parameter.
- Methods are invoked using dot notation.

Ex: if firstStudent is an instance of the StudentType, write

firstStudent.addCredits(3);

Constructing Object Tables

- Ex: Using this new StudentType, can create a new version of the Student table:

```
CREATE TABLE Student of StudentType
(CONSTRAINT Student_stuId_pk PRIMARY KEY(stuId),
CONSTRAINT Student_advisorId_fk FOREIGN KEY
   (advisorId) REFERENCES Faculty (facId));
```

- These are called **object** tables
- They are tables that consist of a single UDT

Inserting Records into an Object Table

- Use the constructor for the UDT
- Ex: Use the StudentType type constructor, as in

INSERT INTO Student

VALUES(**StudentType**('S999', 'Fernandes', 'Luis', 'F101', 0, '25-Jan-1985'));

- Can also insert records in the usual way, without invoking constructor

Using Methods for UDT

- Invoke user-written methods using dot notation:
Ex. StudentType has the addCredits( ) method that we wrote earlier. Invoke by
myStudent.addCredits(3);
- Invoking built-in accessor method:
attribute-name( ) returns the value of the named attribute of a tuple
Ex: to get the first Name of firstStudent:
firstStudent.firstName;()
- Invoking built-in mutator method:
attribute-name(value) assigns the value to the named attribute
Ex: to assign value of 30 to credits of secondStudent:
secondStudent.credits(30);

Type Hierarchies

- Structured types can participate in type hierarchies
- Subtypes inherit attributes and operations, may have additional attributes and operations of their own
- if UDT is FINAL, no subtypes can be defined for it; if NOT FINAL, subtypes allowed
- If class is NOT INSTANTIABLE, cannot create instances of that type, but if it has subtypes, instances of the subtypes can be created, if subtypes are instantiable

EX: Using StudentType, which was NOT FINAL, can define a subtype, UndergraduateType, by writing

CREATE TYPE UndergraduateType UNDER StudentType AS (
major varchar(10) ARRAY[2])
INSTANTIABLE,
NOT FINAL;

- Can create a subtable of Undergraduate type
CREATE TABLE Undergraduate OF UndergraduateType UNDER Student;

UDT Functions, Methods, Procedures

- UDTs and subtypes can have their own methods, functions, and procedures
- Methods have implicit *self* parameter
- Functions do not have implicit parameter, and must have a return type
- Procedures have no return type
  - can have input parameters, identified by the keyword **IN**
  - output parameters, identified by **OUT**
  - two-way parameters, identified by **IN/OUT**
  - Specify before the name of the formal parameter in the procedure heading

Notes

UDT Functions

- Ex: can define a new function, hasDoubleMajor, for the Undergraduate subtype:

```
CREATE FUNCTION hasDoubleMajor (u UndergraduateType)
RETURNS BOOLEAN
BEGIN
    IF (u.major[2] IS NOT NULL)
        THEN
                RETURN TRUE;
        ELSE
                RETURN FALSE;
    END IF;
END;
```

- To use a function in a program, we must provide an actual parameter of UndergraduateType –as in IF (hasDoubleMajor(thirdStudent)) THEN...

UDT Procedures

- Ex:

```
CREATE PROCEDURE countMajors(IN u UndergraduteStudent, OUT
    numberOfMajors SMALLINT)
BEGIN
    numberOfMajors =0;
    IF (u.majors[1] is NOT NULL) THEN numberOfMajors =
                numberOfMajors +1;
    IF (u.majors[2] IS NOT NULL) THEN numberOfMajors =
                numberOfMajors +1;
END;
```

- The procedure would be invoked in statements such as countMajors(fourthStudent, count);
- The output parameter can be used as in

```
IF (count = 2) THEN...
```

Subtypes of Subtypes

- Can create a type called FreshmanType under UndergraduateType

```
CREATE TYPE FreshmanType UNDER
    UndergraduateType AS (
    peerMentor varchar(25))
INSTANTIABLE,
FINAL;
```

- CREATE TABLE Freshmen OF FreshmanType UNDER Undergraduate;

Creating References

- Foreign keys are used to establish relationships between strictly relational tables
- In object-relational tables can have attributes that are actually **references** or pointers to another type, in place of foreign keys
- Ex: Suppose we had already defined FacultyType and a Faculty table of that type. Now we can define StudentType with a reference to the faculty advisor, called aId:

```
CREATE OR REPLACE TYPE StudentType AS (
(stuId            VARCHAR(6),
lastName          VARCHAR(15),
firstName         VARCHAR(12),
aId               REF(FacultyType) SCOPE Faculty,
credits           SMALLINT,
dateOfBirth       DATE)
METHOD            addCredits(smallint);
```

Then to create the Student table, we write
CREATE TABLE Student OF StudentType;

Using Reference Types

- System generates values for references when tuples of the referenced types are inserted
- User must explicitly find and set the reference value when a referencing tuple is inserted
- Ex: To insert Student tuple, first insert with null reference for advisor's aId
INSERT INTO Student VALUES('S555', 'Hughes','John', null, 0,'04-Jan-1988');
- Then update the tuple using a subquery to find reference to the advisor
UPDATE Student
SET aId = (SELECT f.aid
    FROM Faculty AS f
    WHERE facId = 'F101')
WHERE stuId ='S555';
- In queries, can use DEREF operator to find the entire referenced tuple.
SELECT s.lastName, s.firstName, DEREF(s.aid), s.dateOfBirth
FROM Student s
WHERE s.lastName ='Smith';
- Can use the -> operator to retrieve the value of an attribute of the tuple referenced
aId-> lastName
Retrieves the last name of the Faculty advisor
// Note: Oracle uses different method and syntax for references

Converting an E-ER Diagram to an Object-Relational Database

- Entity sets and relationships that are not part of generalizations or unions
  - Proceed as in the relational model
  - Entities map to tables, either using SQL2 syntax or creating a type and using that type for the table
  - For composite attributes, can use ROW type, or define a structured type for the composite, with the components as attributes of the type.
  - Multi-valued attributes use ARRAY
  - For relationships, reference types can be used in place of the foreign key
- For specialization hierarchies, types and subtypes can be defined, and tables and subtables UNDER them to correspond to the types
- **No subtype can have multiple inheritance**
  - choose among potential supertypes for a shared subtype
  - subtype's relationship to other supertype(s) expressed using references or foreign keys
- **No direct representation of unions (categories)**
  - can use the same method as for relational model
    - create a table for the union itself, and individual tables for each of the superclasses, using foreign keys or references to connect them.

Notes

Databases Illuminated

Catherine Ricardo

Databases Illuminated

Chapter 8
The Object-Oriented Model

Why OO?

- Traditional relational model does not represent complex data and relationships well
- Need additional support for advanced applications
- OO paradigm widely used for programming
- OO database provides persistent objects to correspond to temporary objects in programs
- Examples: Objectivity, GemStone, ObjectStore, Versant

OO Data Concepts

- An **object** has a **state** and a unique **identifier**
  - Similar to an entity, but has methods in addition to attributes (data elements)
  - Objects are encapulated – data and methods form a unit with restricted access
  - Only object's methods have access to its data
  - Object's interface is visible to outside world
- A **literal** has a state but no identifier – can be atomic (values of built-in types) or structured

Classes

- A **class** is a set of objects having the same structure-same variables with the same datatypes, same methods, and same relationships
  - Roughly equivalent to an entity type
  - Includes data elements, operations and relationships
  - Datatypes can be predefined atomic types (integer, real, char, boolean), more complex types, or user-defined types
- Set of objects in a class is called the **extent** (like extension)
  - Class extent is roughly equivalent to an entity set
  - Objects in the class (**instances, object instances, objects**) are similar to entity instances

Defining a Class

- Defined by listing components
  - **Data members** (attributes, instance variables)
  - Member **methods** (functions or procedures that belong to the class)
  - **Relationships** that the class participates in

```
Simplified Example:
class Person {
    attribute string name;
    attribute string address;
    attribute string phone;
    void setName(string newName); // method
    string getName( ); //method
    relationship Job hasjob; //relates to Job class
}
```

Writing and Using Methods

- Method written in OO language-Java, C++, etc.
- Ex:

```
void setName(string newName)
{
    self.name = newName;
}
```

- User's program may have a Person object
Person firstPerson = new Person( );
- Invoke method using Person object
firstPerson.setName('Jack Spratt');
- firstPerson becomes "calling object", referred to as *self* in method

Class Hierarchies

- Classes organized into **class hierarchies**
  - **Superclasses (base** classes and **subclasses)**
  - Each subclass has an *isa* relationship with its superclass
- similar to specialization and generalization in the EER model
- Subclasses inherit the data members and methods of their superclasses, and may have additional data members and methods of their own
- Hierarchy diagram-See Figure 8.2
  - Represent classes as rectangles
  - Connect subclasses to *isa* triangle, and connect triangle to superclass

UML Class Diagrams-1

- **Unified Modeling Language (UML)** class diagrams - See Figure 8.5
  - Rectangles for classes- 3 sections: class name, attributes, methods
  - Relationships – 2 types
    - Association
      - for uni- or bi-directional relationships between distinct classes (Ex Student – Faculty relationship)
      - represented by directed line connecting rectangles, with optional name
      - Any descriptive attributes of association in box connected to association line by dotted line (Ex *grade* in Student - ClassSection)
      - Rolenames can appear on line, but placement is opposite that in E-R (Ex. Student *hasAdvisor* role appears next to Faculty)
    - Aggregation
      - Connects parts to a whole, described by "is part of" (Ex ClassSection to Course)
      - Represented by line with diamond on side of aggregate
      - Can be given a name, or interpreted as "has"
  - Reflexive association or reflexive aggregation shown by line back to same class, with rolenames (Ex Course)

UML Diagrams-2

- **Multiplicity indicators** show cardinality & participation
  - min..max, but place opposite to placement in E-R; no ( )
  - Use * for M; use 1 for 1..1
- Generalization hierarchies
  - Lines connect subclasses to superclass, with triangle at end, pointing to superclass
  - Filled triangle for overlapping subclasses
  - Open triangle (outline only) for disjoint subclasses
  - Can write constraints in curly braces on line near triangle (Ex. {overlapping, optional} near Person class rectangle)
- Weak entity represented by rectangle with line to strong entity, with discriminator written in box below strong entity (Ex. *date* is discriminator for Evaluation)

ODMG Model

- Object Database Management Group
- Group of vendors
- Developed standards for OO databases
- Standards for
  - Object model itself
  - **Object definition language** (ODL)
  - **Object query language** (OQL)
  - Language bindings for C++, Java, Smalltalk

ODL-Class Declarations

- See Figure 8.6
- **Class declarations**
  - Begin with word **class**, then *classname*
  - Optional **extent** and **key** declarations in parentheses
  - List of **attributes**, methods, and relationships, all enclosed in curly braces
- **extent**
  - Set of object instances for that class that are stored in the database at a given time; the extension
  - Like the name of the file where the objects in the class are stored

ODL-Attribute Types

- Attribute types – atomic or structured
  - **Atomic types** - integer, float, character, string, boolean, and enumerated types
    - **Enumerated types** - keyword **enum**, name of the type, curly braces with a list of literals for the type, and the name of the attribute with that type
  - Ex: attribute enum FacultyRank{instructor, assistant, associate, professor} rank;

ODL-Structured Types

- Keyword **Struct**, the name of the type, curly braces with each attribute and its datatype, then the identifier of that type

  Ex: **attribute Struct Addr**(string street, string city, string state, string zip) address;

- If type used again for other classes, identify the class it was defined in, using the **scoped name-** class name, double colon, and the type name

  Ex: If we defined Addr type in Person class, and we need a NewAddress field in another class in the same schema, write **attribute newAddress Person::Addr**

Collection Types

- **Set-**finite number of unordered values of one datatype, specified in angled brackets, Set<*typename*>
- **List-**finite list of elements of a single type, written List<*datatype*>
- **Array-**set of elements all of the same type, with an index indicating position of each element; constructor requires datatype and number of elements, as in Array<float, 5>
- **Bag** or multiset-similar to a set, but permits duplicate values, written Bag<*datatype*>
- **Dictionary-**constructor has the form Dictionary <K,V> where K and V are some data types- used to construct pairs of values, <k,v> where k is a key type and v is some range type

Relationships

- Represented by **references**
- System stores and maintains the references
- Ex 1: in Faculty class

  relationship Department belongsTo Inverse Department::hasFaculty;
  - Defines relationship *belongsTo* connecting Faculty to Department
  - A "one" relationship - only one Department reference per Faculty object
  - There is also an inverse relationship *hasFaculty* in Department (bidirectional relationship)
  - Not all relationships have inverses – unidirectional is OK
- Ex 2: in Student class

  relationship Set<ClassSection> takesClass Inverse ClassSection::hasStudent;
  - Defines relationship *takesClass* connecting Student to ClassSection
  - Each Student object has a **set** of references to ClassSection objects-a "many" relationship
- Cardinality of relationship shown by whether or not the word "Set" appears in the relationship specification

Methods

- A function or procedure for members of the class
- Declarations specify the **signature** - the name of the method, the return type (if any), and the number and type of parameters, identified as IN, OUT, or IN/OUT
- Two methods for the same class may have the same name but if their signatures are different, they are different methods
- Actual code for the method is not part of the ODL, but written in a host language
- May be **overloaded** - same method name used for different classes, with different code for them
- Class member methods are applied to an instance of the class

Subclasses

- Keyword **class**, *subclass name*, keyword **extends** *superclass name*

Ex: **class Student extends Person**

- Subclass inherits all attributes, relationships, methods
- Can have additional properties of its own
- For multiple inheritance, add a colon and the name of the second superclass
- Second superclass must be an **interface,** a class definition without an associated extent

Ex: If Student also inherited from a Customer interface
class Student extends Person:Customer

Relationship Classes

- For binary M:M relationships without descriptive attributes, use relationship clause in classes, with Set specification in both directions
- Binary M:M relationships with descriptive attributes
  - Cannot be represented by sets in both directions, since that leaves no place for descriptive attributes
  - Set up a class for the relationship, place the descriptive attributes as attributes of the new class, and define two one-to-many relationships between the new class and the two original classes
  - See **Grade** class in Figure 8.6
- For ternary or higher-order relationships, create a class for the relationship itself
  - New relationship class definition includes three or more relationships that connect the new class to the originally-related classes
  - Also list any descriptive attributes

Keys

- Keys are optional in ODL
- System uses unique object identifier (OID), automatically given to each object instance, to tell instances apart
- Designer can identify any candidate keys as well
- Done at the beginning of the class declaration within the same parentheses as the extent declaration
- Key may be a single attribute or a composite, identified by parentheses around the component attribute names

OQL-Object Query Language-1

- Syntax similar to SQL, but operates on objects, not tables
- Form for queries is
  SELECT *expression list*
  FROM *list of variables*
  WHERE *condition*;
- *expression list* can contain the names of attributes using dot notation, essentially invoking automatic get method, as in
  SELECT s.stuId, s.credits
  FROM students s;
- Can use methods in the expression list –get the result of applying the method
  SELECT p.getName( )
  FROM people p;
- Can use relationship in the expression list- retrieves the object or set of objects related to the calling object through the relationship
  SELECT s.stuId, s.takesClass
  FROM students s
  WHERE s.stuId = 'S999';

OQL-FROM line

- List of variables -similar to defining an alias in SQL
- List the name of an extent, such as students or people, and an identifier for the name of the variable, such as s or p
- Variable is actually an **iterator variable** that ranges over the extent
- Alternate forms for declaring an iterator variable
  FROM students s
  FROM s in students
  FROM students as s

OQL-WHERE line

- Must be boolean expression having constants and variables defined in the FROM clause
- Can use <, <=, >, >=, !=, AND, OR and NOT
- Does not eliminate duplicates; returns a bag
- To eliminate duplicates, add DISTINCT
- Can optionally add ORDER BY

Developing an OO Database

- See Figure 8.7
- Natural extension of application development in an object-oriented programming environment
- Language bindings specified in ODMG standard for C++, Java, and Smalltalk
- Difference between program objects and database objects is **persistence**
- OODBMS provides facilities to make program objects persist, and provides access to database objects for manipulation within programs

Defining the Schema

- Designer defines the schema using a data definition language such as ODL or an OO programming language such as C++
- Class definitions can be standard C++ (or other language) that has been extended to provide persistence and to support relationships between objects, as well as inheritance
- Persistence is provided by making all objects that are to be persistent inherit from a class provided by the OODBMS just for that purpose

Notes

Databases Illuminated

Databases
Illuminated

Catherine Ricardo

Databases Illuminated

Chapter 9
Database Security

Privacy and Security

- Database **security**
  - protecting the database from unauthorized access, modification, or destruction
- **Privacy**
  - the right of individuals to have some control over information about themselves
  - protected by law in many countries
- Right to privacy can be protected by database security

Accidental Security Threats

- User errors
  - User unintentionally requests object or operation for which he/she should not be authorized
- Communications system errors
  - User sent a message that should be sent to another user
  - system connects a user to a session that belongs to another user with different access privileges
- OS errors
  - Accidentally overwrites files and destroys part of database
  - Fetches the wrong files and sends them to the user
  - Fails to erase files that should be erased

Deliberate Security Threats- Sources

- User intentionally gains unauthorized access and/or performs unauthorized operations on the database
- Disgruntled employee who is familiar with the organization's computer system seeks revenge
- Industrial spies seek information for competitors

Deliberate Security Threats- methods

- Wiretapping of communication lines
- Electronic eavesdropping-picking up electronic signals
- Reading display screens or printouts left unsupervised
- Impersonating authorized users or users with greater access
- Writing programs to bypass the DBMS and access database data directly
- Writing applications programs that perform unauthorized operations
- Deriving information about hidden data by clever querying
- Removing physical storage devices from the computer facility
- Making copies of stored files without going through the DBMS
- Bribing, blackmailing or influencing authorized users to obtain information or damage the database

Security Plan

- Should begin with physical security measures for the building-physical barriers, control access, require badges, sign-in etc.
- Should have more physical security for the computer facilities-e.g. locked door
- Additional security control for database

Authentication

- User **authentication -** verifying the identity of users
- Operating system uses user profiles, user ids, passwords, authentication procedures, badges, keys, or physical characteristics of the user
- Additional authentication can be required to access the database-additional user ID, PW

User Profiles

- System has a user profile for each id, giving information about the user
- Stored profiles should be kept secure, possibly in encrypted form
- Profile normally includes a password, allegedly known only to the user
- Passwords should be kept secret and changed frequently
- System should never display passwords at sign-in time

Other Authentication Procedures

- Password limitations-users write them down, choose words that are easy to guess, or share them
- Could require users to insert badges or keys to log on to a workstation
- Voice, fingerprints, retina scans, or other physical characteristics can be used
- Authentication procedure can be series of questions-takes longer and is more difficult to reproduce than PW
- Authentication can be required again at the database
- User should be required to produce an additional PW to access the database

Authorization

- DBMSs designed for multiple users have a security subsystem
- Provide for **authorization**-users are assigned rights to use database objects
- **Authorization language-a**llows the DBA to write **authorization rules** specifying which users have what type of access to database objects

Access Control

- **Access control** covers the mechanisms for implementing authorizations
- **Access control matrix**
  - Planning tool to identify operations different users are permitted to perform on various database objects
  - List users in left column; objects on top row; write operations permitted at intersection
- DBA can delegate authorization powers to others-requires careful planning to avoid abuse

Security Mechanisms

- **Views**-simple method for access control
- **Security log-**journal for storing records of attempted security violations
- **Audit trail**-records all access to the database - requestor, operation performed, workstation used, time, data items and values involved
- **Triggers** can be used to set up an audit trail
- **Encryption** of database data also protects it

Notes

Encryption

- Uses a **cipher system** that consists of
  - **Encryption algorithm** that converts **plaintext** into **ciphertext**
  - **Uses encrypting key**
  - **Decryption algorithm** that reproduces plaintext from ciphertext
  - **Uses decryption key**
- Widely-used schemes for encryption
  - **Data Encryption Standard (DES)** and **Advanced Encryption Standard (AES)**
    - uses a standard algorithm, which is often hardware implemented
  - **Public key encryption**-uses a product of primes as a public key, and the prime factors of the product as a private key
    - Ex. **RSA**, named for its developers Rivest, Shamir and Adleman

DES and AES

- **Data Encryption Standard-DES** See Figure 9.4
  - National Bureau of Standards, 1977
  - Algorithm is public-can have hardware implementation
  - Key is private
  - Uses **symmetric** encryption-decryption key is the same as the encryption key and decryption algorithm is the inverse of encryption algorithm
  - Uses 56-bit key on 64-bit blocks of plaintext, producing 64-bit blocks of ciphertext
  - In each block, characters are substituted and rearranged according to the value of the key
  - Two major challenges with the DES system: key security and ease of cracking the code
- **Advanced Encryption Standard-AES**
  - Developed in 2000
  - symmetric scheme; more sophisticated than the DES scheme
  - three key sizes-128s,192, or 256 bits, depending on the level of security needed
  - Due to larger key sizes, cracking the scheme is more challenging

SQL Authorization Language

- GRANT statement used for authorization
- REVOKE statement used to retract authorization
- Privileges can be given to users directly
- Privileges can also be given to a role, and role given to users
- System keeps track of authorizations using a **grant diagram,** also called an **authorization graph**
- In Oracle, privileges include **object privileges** and **system privileges**
  - Granted using the authorization sublanguage or through the Oracle Security Manage

GRANT Statement

GRANT {ALL PRIVILEGES | *privilege-list*}
ON   {*table-name*|*view-name*}
TO {PUBLIC | *user-list*|*role-list*} [WITH GRANT OPTION];
- privileges for base tables are SELECT, DELETE, INSERT, UPDATE or REFERENCES(*col-name*)
- For updatable views, privileges are SELECT, DELETE, INSERT and UPDATE
- To grant privileges to a user-Ex.
GRANT SELECT ON Student TO U101 WITH GRANT OPTION;
- To create and use a role-Ex.
  - CREATE ROLE AdvisorRole;
  - Grant privileges to the role
    - GRANT SELECT ON Student TO AdvisorRole;
  - Assign a role to a user
    - GRANT AdvisorRole to U999;
  - To assign a role to another role
    - GRANT FacultyRole TO AdvisorRole;
    - Allows inheritance of role privileges

REVOKE

- REVOKE {ALL PRIVILEGES | *privilege-list*}
ON *object-list*
FROM {PUBLIC | *user-list* | *role-list*}
[*CASCADE* | *RESTRICT*];

- Ex:
  - REVOKE INSERT ON Student FROM U101;
- Can revoke just the grant option, without revoking the underlying privilege,
  - REVOKE GRANT OPTION FOR INSERT ON Student FROM U101;
- By default, revocations **cascade** or trigger other revocations, if the user has passed on the privileges that are revoked
- If RESTRICT is specified, any revocation that would cascade to others will not be performed

Statistical Databases

- Support statistical analysis on populations
- Data itself may contain facts about individuals, but is not meant to be retrieved on an individual basis
- Users are permitted to access statistical information-totals, counts, or averages, but not information about individuals

Statistical DB Security

- Need special precautions to ensure users are not able to deduce data about individuals
- Even if all queries must involve count, sum or average, user can use conditions in WHERE line to narrow the population down to one individual
- System can refuse any query for which only one record satisfies the predicate-not sufficient protection
- Can restrict queries
  - Require that the number of records satisfying the predicate be above some threshold
  - Require that the number of records satisfying a pair of queries simultaneously cannot exceed some limit
  - Can disallow sets of queries that repeatedly involve the same records

Need for DB Security on the Internet

- Messages transmitted in plaintext can be read by intruders using packet sniffing software
- Customers need assurance their credit card info is kept private when sent over the Internet
- Companies that allow web connections to their internal networks for access to their database need to protect it from attack
- Receivers and senders of messages need to be sure that the site they are communicating with is genuine and trustworthy

Techniques for Internet Security

- Firewalls
- Certifications authorities such as Verisign that issue digital certificates using SSL or S-HTTP
- SET for financial information
- Digital signatures

Firewalls

- A hardware/software barrier that protects an organization's intranet from unauthorized access
- Ensures that messages entering or leaving intranet meet the organization's standards
- May use a **proxy server** that intercepts all messages in both directions-hides the actual network address
- **Packet filter** examines each packet of information before it enters or leaves the intranet
- Gateway techniques can apply security mechanisms to applications or connections

Certification Authorities-SSL & S-HTTP

- **Verisign**-method of verifying that a site is genuine
- Uses public key encryption
- **Secure Sockets Layer** (SSL) protocol
  - site begins process by generating a public key and a private key, and sending a request to Verisign, along with the site's public key
  - Verisign issues an encrypted certificate to the site
  - Customer browser asks the site for its Verisign certificate; receives it in encrypted form
  - Browser decrypts the certificate using Verisign's public key, verifies that this is a Verisign certificate, and that the site's URL is the correct one
  - Certificate also contains the site's public key
  - Browser creates a session key, encrypts it using the site's public key from the certificate, and sends the session key to the site
  - Only the actual site can decrypt it using its private key
  - Browser and the site are the sole holders of the session key; they can exchange messages encrypted with it, using simpler protocol- DES or AES
- **Secure HTTP** (S-HTTP), similar to SSL-guarantees security of individual messages rather than an entire session

SET

- **Secure Electronic Transaction** (SET) protocol
- Provides additional security for credit card info
- When customer is ready to transmit order info, browser sends the site most of the order information encoded with its public key
- Credit card information is encoded with the public key of the credit card company, so site cannot decode it directly
- Site sends credit card information directly to the card company site for approval and payment

Notes

Digital Signatures

- Double form of public key encryption
- Creates secure two-way communications that cannot be repudiated
- Users can verify the authenticity of the person they are communicating with, and prove that a message must have come from that person
- Sender encodes a message first with his or her own private key, and then with the public key of the receiver
- Receiver decrypts the message first using his or her private key, and then using the sender's public key
- Double encryption ensures that both parties are authentic, since neither one could have encoded or decoded the message without his or her private key
- Variation uses a Certification Authority, similar to SSL

Notes

Databases Illuminated

Chapter 10
Transaction Management

Protecting the Database During Transactions

- **Recovery-**restoring the database to a correct state after a failure
- **Concurrency control-**allows simultaneous use of the database without having users interfere with one another
- Both protect the database

Steps in a Transaction

- Simple update of one record:
  - Locate the record to be updated
  - Bring the block into the buffer
  - Write the update to buffer
  - Write the modified block out to disk
- More complicated transactions may involve several updates
- Modified buffer block may not be written to disk immediately after transaction terminates-must assume there is a delay before actual write is done

Basic Ideas About Transactions

- **Transaction**- a logical unit of work that takes the database from one consistent state to another
- Transactions can terminate successfully and **commit** or unsuccessfully and be **aborted**
- Aborted transactions must be undone (**rolled back**) if they changed the database
- Committed transactions cannot be rolled back
- See Figure 10.2 - transaction state diagram

ACID Properties of Transactions

- **Atomicity**
  - Single "all or none" unit; entire set of actions carried out or none are
  - DBMS must roll back-UNDO- transactions that will not be able to complete successfully
  - **Log** of transactions' writes used in the rollback process
- **Consistency**
  - Users responsible for ensuring that each transaction, executed individually, leaves the database in a consistent state
  - Concurrency control subsystem must ensure this for multiple transactions
- **Isolation**
  - When transactions execute simultaneously, DBMS ensures that the final effect is as if the transactions were executed one after another (serially)
- **Durability**
  - Effect of any committed transaction is permanently recorded in the database, even if the system crashes before all its writes are made to the database
  - Recovery subsystem must guarantee durability

Concurrency Problems

- Concurrency control needed when transactions are permitted to process simultaneously, if at least one is an update
- Potential problems due to lack of concurrency control:
  - **Lost update problem**-Figure 10.3
  - **Uncommitted update problem**-Figure 10.4
  - **Inconsistent analysis problem**-Figure 10.5
  - **Nonrepeatable read problem**-first transaction reads an item; second transaction writes a new value for the item; first transaction rereads the item and gets a different value
  - **Phantom data problem**- first transaction reads a set of rows; second transaction inserts a row; first transaction reads the rows again and sees the new row

Conflict in Transactions

- If two transactions are only reading data items, they do not conflict and order is not important
- If two transactions operate on completely separate data items, they do not conflict and order is not important
- If one transaction writes to a data item and another either reads or writes to the same data item, then the order of execution is important
- Therefore, two operations **conflict** only if **all** of these are true
  - they belong to different transactions
  - they access the same data item
  - at least one of them writes the item

Serial vs Interleaved Execution

- **Interleaved execution** – control goes back and forth between operations of two or more transactions
- **Serial execution-** execute one transaction at a time, with no interleaving of operations. Ex. A, then B
  - Can have more than one possible serial execution for two or more transactions –Ex:A,B or B,A
  - For n transactions, there are n! possible serial executions
  - They may not all produce the same results
  - However, DB considers all serial executions to be correct
- See Figure 10.6

Serializable Schedules

- A **schedule** is used to show the timing of the operations of one or more transaction
- Shows the order of operations
- Schedule is **serializable** if it produces the same results as if the transactions were performed serially in some order
- Objective is to find serializable schedules to maximize concurrency while maintaining correctness

Conflict Serializability

- If schedule orders any conflicting operations in the same way as some serial execution the results of the concurrent execution are the same as the results of that serial schedule
- This type of serializability is called **conflict serializability**

Precedence Graph

- Used to determine whether a schedule, S, is conflict serializable
- Draw a node for each transaction, T1, T2, …Tn. For the schedule, draw directed edges as follows
  - If Ti writes X, and then Tj reads X, draw edge from Ti to Tj
  - If Ti reads X, and then Tj writes X, draw edge from Ti to Tj
  - If Ti writes X, and then Tj writes X, draw edge from Ti to Tj
- S is **conflict serializable** if graph has **no cycles**
- If S is serializable, can use the graph to find an equivalent serial schedule by examining the edges
  - If an edge appears from Ti to Tj, put Ti before Tj
  - If several nodes appear on the graph, you usually get a partial ordering of graph
  - May be several possible serial schedules

Methods to Ensure Serializability

- **Locking**
- **Timestamping**
- Concurrency control subsystem is "part of the package" and not directly controllable by either the users or the DBA
- A **scheduler** is used to allow operations to be executed immediately, delayed, or rejected
- If an operation is delayed, it can be done later by the same transaction
- If an operation is rejected, the transaction is aborted but it may be restarted later

Locks

- Transaction can ask DBMS to place locks on data items in the DB
- Lock prevents another transaction from modifying the object
- Transactions may wait until locks are released before their lock requests can be granted
- Objects of various sizes (DB, table, page, record, data item) can be locked.
- Size determines the fineness, or **granularity**, of the lock
- Lock implemented by inserting a flag in the object or by keeping a list of locked parts of the database
- Locks can be **exclusive** or **shared** by transactions
  - Shared locks are sufficient for read-only access
  - Exclusive locks are necessary for write access
- Figure 10.8 – lock compatibility matrix

Deadlock

- Often, transaction cannot specify in advance exactly what records it will need to access in either its **read set** or its **write set**
- **Deadlock** - two or more transactions wait for locks being held by each another
- Deadlock detection uses a **wait-for** graph to identify deadlock
  - Draw a node for each transaction
  - If transaction S is waiting for a lock held by T, draw an edge from S to T
- **Cycle** in the graph shows deadlock
- Deadlock is resolved by choosing a **victim**-newest transaction or one with least resources
- Should avoid always choosing the same transaction as the victim, a situation called **starvation**, because that transaction will never complete

Two-phase locking protocol

- A protocol that guarantees serializability
- Every transaction acquires all its locks before releasing any, but not necessarily all at once
- Transaction has two phases:
  - In **growing** phase, transaction obtains locks
  - In **shrinking** phase, it releases locks
- Once it enters its shrinking phase, can never obtain a new lock
- For **standard two-phase locking**, the rules are
  - Transaction must acquire a lock on an item before operating on the item. For read-only access, a shared lock is sufficient. For write access, an exclusive lock is required.
  - Once the transaction releases a single lock, it can never acquire any new locks
- Deadlock can still occur

Cascading Rollbacks

- **Cascading rollback**.
  - Locks can be released before COMMIT in standard two-phase locking protocol
  - An uncommitted transaction may be rolled back after releasing its locks
  - If a second transaction has read a value written by the rolled back transaction, it must also roll back, since it read **dirty data**
- **Avoiding cascading rollback**
  - **Strict** two phase locking: transactions hold their exclusive locks until COMMIT, preventing cascading rollbacks
  - **Rigorous** two-phase locking: transactions hold all locks, both shared and exclusive, until COMMIT

Lock Upgrading and Downgrading

- Transaction may at first request shared locks-allow other transactions concurrent read access to the items
- When transaction ready to do an update, requests that the shared lock be **upgraded**, converted into an exclusive lock
- Upgrading can take place only during the growing phase, and may require that the transaction wait until another transaction releases a shared lock on the item
- Once an item has been updated, its lock can be **downgraded**, converted from exclusive to shared mode
- Downgrading can take place only during the shrinking phase.

Intention Locking

- Can represent database objects as a hierarchy by size
- Root node is the entire DB, level 1 nodes tables, level 2 nodes pages, level 3 nodes records, level 4 data items
- If a node is locked, all its descendants are also locked
- If a second transaction requests an incompatible lock on the **same** node, system knows that the lock cannot be granted
- If second transaction requests a lock on any descendant, system checks to see if any of its **ancestors** are locked before deciding whether to grant the lock
- If a transaction requests a lock on a node when a **descendant** is already locked, we don't want to search too much to determine this
- Need an **intention** lock, which may be shared or exclusive-shows some descendant is probably locked
- Two-phase protocol is used
  - No lock can be granted once any node has been unlocked
  - No node may be locked until its parent is locked by an intention lock
  - No node may be unlocked until all its descendants are unlocked
- Apply locking from the root down, using intention locks until the node is reached, and release locks from leaves up
- Deadlock is still possible

Notes

Timestamping

- Each transaction has a timestamp; gives the relative order of the transaction
- Timestamp could be clock reading or logical counter
- Each data item has
  - a **Read-Timestamp**-timestamp of last transaction that read the item
  - **Write-Timestamp**-timestamp of last transaction that wrote the item
- Problems
  - Transaction tries to read an item already updated by a younger transaction (late read)
  - Transaction tries to write an item already updated by a later transaction (late write)
- protocol takes care of these problems by rolling back transactions that cannot execute correctly

Basic Timestamping Protocol

Compare TS(T) with WriteTimestamp(P) and/or ReadTimestamp(P) which identify the transaction(s) that last wrote or read the data item, P
1. If T asks to **read** P, compare TS(T) with WriteTimestamp(P)
   - (a) If WriteTimestamp(P) <= TS(T) then proceed using the current data value and replace ReadTimestamp(P) with TS(T). However, if ReadTimestamp(P) is already larger than TS(T), just do the read and do not change ReadTimestamp(P)
   - (b) If WriteTimestamp(P) > TS(T), then T is late doing its read, and the value of P that it needs is already overwritten, so roll back T
2. If T asks to **write** P, compare TS(T) with both Write-Timestamp(P) and the Read-Timestamp(P)
   - (a) If Write-Timestamp(P) <= TS(T) and Read-Timestamp(P) <= TS(T), do the write and replace WriteTimestamp(P) with TS(T)
   - (b) else roll back T, assign a new timestamp, and restart T

Thomas' Write Rule

- Variation of the basic timestamping protocol that allows greater concurrency
- Applies when T is trying to write P, but new value has already been written for P by a younger transaction
- If a younger transaction has already **read** P, then it needed the value that T is trying to write, so roll back T and restart it
- Otherwise ignore T's write of P, and let T proceed

Multiversioning

- Concurrency can be increased if we allow multiple versions of data items to be stored
- Transactions can access the version that is consistent for them
- Data item P has a sequence of versions <P1, P2, ..., Pn>, each of which has
  - The content field, a value for Pi,
  - Write-Timestamp(Pi), timestamp of transaction that wrote the value
  - Read-Timestamp(Pi), timestamp of youngest transaction that has read version Pi
- When write(P) is done, a new version of P is created, with appropriate write-timestamp
- When read(P) is done, the system selects the appropriate version of P.

Multiversion Timestamp Protocol

- When T does a read(P)
  - Value used is the value of the content field associated with the latest Write-Timestamp that is less than or equal to TS(T)
  - Read-Timestamp is set to later of TS(T) or current value
- When T does a write(P)
  - Version used is the one whose write timestamp is the largest one that is less than or equal to TS(T)
  - For that version
    - If Read-Timestamp(P) > TS(T), P has already been read by a younger transaction, so roll back T, since it would be a late write
    - Else create a new version of P, with read and write timestamps TS(T)

Validation Techniques

- Also called **optimistic** techniques
- Assume that conflict will be rare
- Transactions proceed as if there were no concurrency problems
- Before a transaction commits perform check to determine whether a conflict has occurred
- If there is a conflict, the transaction must be rolled back
- Assume rollback will be rare
- Rollback is the price to be paid for eliminating locks
- No cascading rollbacks, since writes are to local copy only
- Allow more concurrency, since no locking is done

Phases in Validation Techniques

- Transaction goes through two phases for read-only, three for updating:
  - **Read** phase, from transaction's start until just before it commits
    - reads all the variables it needs, stores them in local variables
    - Does any writes to a local copy of the data, not to the database
  - **Validation** phase, follows the read phase
    - Tests to determine whether there is any interference
    - For read-only transaction, checks to see that there was no error due to another transaction active when the data values were read. If no error, the transaction is committed. If interference occurred, the transaction is aborted and restarted
    - For a transaction that does updates, checks whether the current transaction will leave the database in a consistent state, with serializability. If not, the transaction is aborted..
  - **write** phase, follows successful validation phase for update transaction
    - The updates made to the local copy are applied to the database

Validation Phase

- Examines reads and writes of other transactions, T, that may cause interference
- Each other transaction, T, has three timestamps
  - Start(T), the relative starting time of the transaction
  - Validation(T), given at the end of its read phase as it enters its validation phase
  - Finish(T), its finishing time, the time it finished (including its write phase, if any)
- To pass the validation test, **one** of the following must be true:
1. All transactions with earlier timestamps must have finished (including their writes) before the current transaction started **OR**
2. If the current transaction starts before earlier one finishes, then **both** of these are true

   a) the items written by the earlier transaction are not the ones read by the current transaction, **and**

   b) the earlier transaction completes its write phase before the current transaction enters its validation phase

- Rule (a) guarantees that the writes of the earlier transaction are not read by the current transaction; rule (b) guarantees that the writes are done serially

Need for Recovery

- Many different types of failures that can affect database processing
- Some causes of failure
  - Natural physical disasters
  - Sabotage
  - Carelessness
  - Disk malfunctions- result in loss of stored data
  - System crashes due to hardware malfunction-result in loss of main and cache memory
  - System software errors-result in abnormal termination or damage to the DBMS
  - Applications software errors

Possible Effects of Failure

- Loss of main memory, including database buffers
- Loss of the disk copy of the database

- DBMS recovery subsystem uses techniques that minimize these effects

Recovery Manager

- DBMS subsystem responsible for ensuring **atomicity** and **durability** for transactions in the event of failure
  - Atomicity-all of a transaction is performed or none
    - Recovery manager ensures that all the effects of committed transactions reach the database, and that the effects of any uncommitted transactions are undone
  - Durability-effects of a committed transaction are permanent
    - Effects must survive both loss of main memory and loss of disk storage

Loss of Disk Data

- Handled by doing frequent backups-making copies of the database
- In case of disk failure, the backup can be brought up to date using a log of transactions

System Failure

- If system failure occurs
  - Database buffers are lost
  - Disk copy of the database survives, but it may be incorrect
- A transaction can commit once its writes are made to the database buffers
- Updates made to buffer are not automatically written to disk, even for committed transactions
- May be a delay between commit and actual disk writing
- If system fails during this delay, we must ensure that these updates reach the disk copy of the database

Recovery Log

- Contains records of each transaction showing
  - The start of transaction
  - Write operations of transaction
  - End of transaction
- If system fails, the log is examined to see what transactions to **redo** and/or what transactions to **undo**
- Several different protocols are used

Deferred Update Protocol

- DBMS does all database writes in the log, and does not write to the database until the transaction is ready to commit
- Uses the log to protect against system failures :
  - When transaction starts, write a record of the form <T starts> to the log
  - When a write is performed, do not write the update to the database buffers or the database itself. Instead, write a log record of the form <T,X, n>
  - When a transaction is about to commit, write a log record of the form <T commits>, write all the log records for the transaction to disk, and then commit the transaction. Use the log records to perform the updates to the database buffers. Later, these updates pages will be written to disk
  - If the transaction aborts, simply ignore the log records for the transaction and do not perform the writes.
  - Called a **redo/no undo** method since we redo committed transactions and don't undo anything

Notes

Checkpoints

- After a failure, we may not know how far back in the log to search for redo of transactions
- Can limit log searching using **checkpoints**
- Scheduled at predetermined intervals
- Checkpoint operations
  - Write modified blocks in the database buffers to disk
  - Write a checkpoint record to the log-contains the names of all transactions that are active at the time of the checkpoint
  - Write all log records now in main memory out to disk

Using Checkpoint Records

- When a failure occurs, check the log
- If transactions are performed serially
  - Find the last transaction that started before the last checkpoint
  - Any earlier transaction would have committed previously and would have been written to the database at the checkpoint
  - Need only redo the one that was active at the checkpoint (provided it committed) and any subsequent transactions for which both start and commit records appear in the log
- If transactions are performed concurrently
  - Checkpoint record contains the names of **all** transactions that were active at checkpoint time
  - Redo all those transactions (if they committed) and all subsequent ones that committed

Immediate Update Protocol

- Updates are applied to the database buffers as they occur and written to the database itself when convenient
- A log record is written first, since this is a **write-ahead** log protocol
- Protocol
  - When a transaction starts, write a record of the form <T starts> to the log
  - When a write operation is performed, write a log record with the name of the transaction, the field name, the old value, and the new value of the field. This has the form <T,X,o,n>
  - After writing log record, write the update to the database buffers
  - When convenient, write the log records to disk and then write updates to the database itself
  - When the transaction commits, write a record of the form <T commits> to the log

Using the Immediate Update Log

- If a transaction aborts, use log to **undo** it, since it contains all the old values for the updated fields
  - Writes are undone in reverse order
  - Writing the old values means the database will be restored to its state prior to the start of the transaction
- If the system fails
  - In recovery, use the log to **undo** or **redo** transactions, making this a **redo/undo** protocol
  - For any transaction, T, for which both <T starts> and <T commits> records appear in the log, **redo** by using the log records to write the new values of updated fields-any write that did not actually reach the database will now be performed
  - For any transaction, S, for which the log contains an <S starts> record, but not an <S commits> record, need to **undo** - log records are used to write the old values of the affected fields, in reverse order

Shadow Paging-Page Tables

- Alternative to logging
- DBMS has a **page table** with pointers to all current database pages
- Keeps both a **current page table** and a **shadow page table**, which are initially identical
- All modifications are made to the current page table-shadow table is left unchanged
- To modify a database page, system finds an unused page on disk, copies the old database page to the new one, and makes changes to the new page
- Updates the current page table to point to the new page

Shadow Paging-Transaction End

- If the transaction completes successfully, current page table becomes the shadow page table
  - Write all modified pages from the database buffers to disk
  - Copy the current page table to disk
  - In the location on disk where the address of the shadow page table is recorded, write the address of the current page table, making it the new shadow page table
- If the transaction fails, new pages are ignored; shadow page table becomes the current page table

ARIES Recovery Technique

- Flexible and conceptually simple method for recovery
- Each log record is given a unique **log sequence number** (LSN), assigned in increasing order
- Each log record records the LSN of the previous log record for the same transaction, forming a linked list
- Each database page has a **pageLSN**, the LSN of the last log record that updated it
- **Transaction table** has an entry for each active transaction, with the transaction identifier, the status (active, committed or aborted), and the **lastLSN**, the LSN of the latest log record for the transaction
- **Dirty page table** has an entry for each page in the buffer that has been updated but not yet written to disk, and the **recLSN**, the LSN of the oldest log record for any update to the buffer page
- Uses write-ahead logging-log record is written to disk before any database disk update
- Does checkpointing to limit log searching in recovery

ARIES Recovery Protocol

- Tries to repeat history during recovery-repeats all database actions done before the crash, even those of incomplete transactions
- Does redo and undo as needed
- Three phases
  - **Analysis:** begins with most recent checkpoint record, reads forward in the log to identify which transactions were active at the time of failure; uses transaction table and dirty page table to determine which buffer pages contain updates not yet written to disk; determines how far back in the log it needs to go to recover, using the linked lists of LSNs
  - **Redo:** from starting point in the log identified during analysis, goes forward in the log, applies all the unapplied updates from the log records
  - **Undo:** going backwards from the end of the log, undoes updates done by uncommitted transactions, ending at the oldest log record of any transaction that was active at the time of the crash

Oracle Transaction Management

- Multiversion concurrency control mechanism, with no read locks
- For read-only transactions, uses a consistent view of the database at the point in time when it began, including only those updates that were committed at that time
- Creates **rollback segments** that contain the older versions of data items-used for both read consistency and undo operations that may be needed
- Uses type of timestamp called a **system change number** (SCN) given to each transaction at its start

Oracle Concurrency Control

- Several types of locks available, including both DML and DDL locks
- DDL locks are applied at the table level
- DML locks are at the row-level
- Uses a deadlock detection scheme, and rolls back one of the transactions if needed
- Provides two **isolation levels**, degrees of protection from other transactions
  - **Read committed:** default level-guarantees that each statement in a transaction reads only data committed before the statement started. Since data may be changed during the transaction, there may be nonrepeatable reads and phantom data.
  - **Serializable:** gives transaction-level consistency-ensures that a transaction sees only data committed before the transaction started

Oracle Recovery

- **Recovery manager** (RMAN) is a GUI tool that the DBA can use to control backup and recovery operations
- RMAN can make backups of the database or parts of it, backups of recovery logs, can restore data from backups, can perform recovery operations of redo, undo
- Maintains control files, rollback segments, redo logs, and archived redo logs
- When a redo log is filled, it can be archived automatically
- Can also provide a managed standby database
  - Copy of the operational database kept at another location
  - Takes over if the regular database fails
  - Kept nearly up to date by shipping the archived redo logs and applying the updates to the standby database

Notes

Databases Illuminated

Catherine Ricardo

Databases Illuminated

Chapter 11
Query Optimization

Query processing overview

- Steps in executing SQL query-DBMS:
  - Checks query syntax
  - Validates query-checks data dictionary; verifies objects referred to are database objects and requested operations are valid
  - Translates query into relational algebra (or relational calculus)
  - Rearranges relational algebra operations into most efficient form
  - Uses its knowledge of table size, indexes, order of tuples, distribution of values, to determine how the query will be processed-estimates the "cost" of alternatives and chooses the plan with the least estimated cost-considers the number of disk accesses, amount of memory, processing time, and communication costs, if any
  - Execution plan is then coded and executed
  - Figure 11.1 summarizes this process

Relational Algebra Translation

- SQL Select..From..Where usually translates into combination of RA SELECT, PROJECT, JOIN
- RA SELECT-unary operator: s_p(*table-name*)
  - p is a predicate, called the _ (theta) condition
  - Returns entire rows that satisfy _
- RA PROJECT-unary operator: $P_{proj-list}$(*table-name*)
  - Proj-list is a list of columns
  - Returns unique combinations of values for those columns
- RA JOIN-binary operator: *table1* |X| *table2*
  - Compares table1 and table2, which have a common column (or columns with same domain)
  - Chooses rows from each that match on common column
  - Combines those rows, but shows common column only once

Query Tree

- Graphical representation of the operations and operands in relational algebra expression
- Leaf nodes are relations
- Unary or binary operations are internal nodes
- An internal node can be executed when its operands are available
- Node is replaced by the result of the operation it represents
- Root node is executed last, and is replaced by the result of the entire tree
- See Figure 11.2

Doing SELECT early

- Same SQL statement can be translated to different relational algebra statements
- Performing SELECT early reduces size of intermediate nodes-See Figure 11.2(b)
- Push SELECT as far down the tree as possible
- For conjunctive SELECT, do each part on its own tree instead of waiting for join-See Figure 11.3(b)

Some Properties of Natural JOIN

- Associative
  - (Student |x| Enroll) |x| Class same as
  - Student |x| (Enroll |x| Class)
- Commutative, ignoring column order
  - Enroll |x| Class ∫ Class |x| Enroll

Many similar rules exist

RA Equivalences-1

1. *All joins and products are commutative.*
   R ¥ S ∫ S ¥ R and
   R |¥| q S ∫ S |¥|q R and
   R |¥| S ∫ S |¥| R
2. *Joins and products are associative*
   (R ¥ S) ¥ T ∫ R ¥ (S ¥ T)
   (R |¥|q S) |¥|q T ∫ R |¥|q (S |¥|q T)
   (R |¥| S) |¥| T ∫ R |¥| (S |¥| T)

RA Equivalences-2

3. *Select is commutative*
   $s_p (s_q (R)) \int s_q (s_p (R))$
4. *Conjunctive selects can cascade into individual selects*
   $s_{p\&q\&...\&z} (R) \int (s_p (s_q...(s_z (R))...))$
5. *Successive projects can reduced to the final project.*
   If list1, list2, … listn are lists of attribute names and each of the list*i* contains list*i-1*, then
   $P_{list1} (P_{list2} (...P_{listn} (R)...) \int P_{list1}(R)$
   • So only the last project has to be executed

RA Equivalences-3

6. *Select and project sometimes commute*
   • If p involves only the attributes in projlist, then select and project commute
   $P_{projlist} (s_p (R)) \int s_p (P_{projlist} (R))$
7. *Select and join (or product) sometimes commute*
   • If p involves only attributes of one of the tables being joined, then select and join commute
   $s_p (R |¥| S) \int (s_p (R)) |¥| S$
   • Only if p refers just to R

RA Equivalences-4

8. **Select sometimes distributes over join (or product)**
   - For p AND q, where p involves only the attributes of R and q only the attributes of S the select distributes over the join
   $s_{p\ ANDq}\ (R\ |¥|\ S)\ \int\ (\ s_p\ (R))\ |¥|\ (\ s_q\ (S))$

9. **Project sometimes distributes over join (or product)**
   - If projlist can be split into separate lists, list1 and list2, so that list1 contains only attributes of R and list2 contains only attributes of S, then
   $P_{projlist}\ (R\ |¥|\ S)\ \int\ (\ P_{list1}\ (R))\ |¥|\ (\ P_{list2}\ (S))$

RA Equivalences-5

10. **Union and intersection are commutative**
    $R » S \int S » R$
    $R \_ S \int S \_ R$
    - Set difference is not commutative.

11. **Union and intersection are individually associative.**
    $(R » S) » T \int R » (S » T)$
    $(R \_ S) \_ T \int R \_ (S \_ T)$
    - Set difference is not associative

RA Equivalences-6

12. **Select distributes over union, intersection, and difference**
    $s_p\ (R » S) \int s_p\ (R) » s_p\ (S)$
    $s_p\ (R \_ S) \int s_p\ (R) \_ s_p\ (S)$
    $s_p\ (R - S) \int s_p\ (R) - s_p\ (S)$

13. **Project distributes over union, intersection, and difference**
    $P_{projlist}\ (R » S) \int (P_{projlist}\ (R)) » (P_{projlist}\ (S))$
    $P_{projlist}\ (R \_ S) \int (P_{projlist}\ (R)) \_ P_{projlist}\ (S))$
    $P_{projlist}\ (R - S) \int (P_{projlist}\ (R)) - (P_{projlist}\ (S))$

14. **Project is idempotent-repeating it produces the same result**
    $P_{projlist}\ (R)(\ P_{projlist}(R))\ \int P_{projlist}(R)$

15. **Select is idempotent**
    $s_p(s_p(R))\ \int s_p\ (R)$

Heuristics for Optimization

- **Do selection as early as possible.** Use cascading, commutativity, and distributivity to move selection as far down the query tree as possible
- Use associativity to rearrange relations so the selection operation that will produce the smallest table will be executed first
- If a product appears as an argument for a selection, where the selection involves attributes of the tables in the product, change the product to a join
  - If the selection involves attributes of only one of the tables in the product, apply the selection to that table first
- **Do projection early.** Use cascading, distributivity and commutativity to move the projection as far down the query tree as possible.
- Examine all projections to see if some are unnecessary
- If a sequence of selections and/or projections have the same argument, use commutativity or cascading to combine them into one selection, one projection, or a selection followed by a projection
- If a subexpression appears more than once in the query tree, and the result it produces is not too large, compute it once and save it

Cost Factors

- Cost factors of executing a query
  - Cost of reading files
  - Processing costs once data is in main memory
  - Cost of writing and storing intermediate results
  - Communication costs
  - Cost of writing final results to storage
- Most significant factor is the number of disk accesses, the read and write costs
- System uses statistics stored in the data dictionary and knowledge about the size, structure and access methods of each file

Estimating Access Cost

- **Access cost**-number of blocks brought into main memory for reading or written to secondary storage as result
- Tables may be stored in
  - **packed form**-blocks contain only tuples from one table
  - **unpacked form**, tuples are interspersed with tuples from other tables
- If unpacked, have to assume every tuple of relation is in a different block
- If packed, estimate the number of blocks from tuple size, number of tuples, and capacity of the block
- Some useful symbols:
  - $t(R)$, number of tuples in relation R
  - $b(R)$, number of blocks needed to store R
  - $bf(R)$, number of tuples of R per block, called **blocking factor** of R
  - **If R is packed, then $b(R) = t(R)/bf(R)$**
- Example: If the Student relation has blocks of 4K bytes, and there are 10,000 student records each 200 bytes long, then 20 records fit per block (4096/200). We need 10000/20 or 500 blocks to hold this file in packed form

Access Paths for a Table

- May be in order by key (primary or secondary)
- May be hashed on the value of a primary key
- May have an index on the primary key, and/or secondary indexes on non-primary-key attributes

Indexes

- May be **clustered index**, tuples with the same value of the index appear in the same block-one per table. Other indexes will then be **nonclustered**
- May be **dense**, having an entry for each tuple of the relation, or **nondense**
- Normally **B+ tree** or a similar structure is used
- Must first access the index itself, so cost of accessing the index must be considered, in addition to data access
- Index access cost is usually small compared to the cost of accessing the data records

Symbols for Cost of Using Indexes

- l(index-name), the number of levels in a multi-level index, or the average number of index accesses needed to find an entry
- n(A,R), the number of distinct values of attribute A in relation R
- If the values of A are **uniformly distributed** in R, then the number of tuples expected to have a particular value, c, for A, the **selection size** or s(A=c,R), is

  $s(A=c,R) = t(R)/n(A,R)$
  - if A is a candidate key, each tuple has a unique value for A, so $n(A,R) = t(R)$ and the selection size is 1

Example

- Estimate the number of students in the university with a major of Mathematics
  - If there are 10,000 students, t(Student) =10000
  - If there are 25 major subjects, n(major, Student) = 25
  - Then number of Mathematics majors is

s(major='Math',Student) = t(Student)/n(major,Student) = 10000/25 = 400

- We assume majors are uniformly distributed, that the number of students choosing each major is about equal
- Some systems use **histograms**, graphs that show the frequencies of different values of attributes. The histogram gives a more accurate estimate of the selection size for a particular value
- Some systems store the minimum and maximum values for each attribute

Estimating Cost for SELECT, $s_{A=c}(R)$

- Depends on what access paths exist
  - If file hashed on the selection attribute(s)
  - If file has an index on the attribute(s) and whether the index is clustered
  - If file is in order by the selection attribute(s)
  - If none of the above applies

Full Table Scan

- "Worst case" method-always compare other methods to this one
- Used when there is no access path for the attribute
- Cost is the number of blocks in the table-have to examine every tuple in the table to see if it qualifies
- Cost is **b(R)**

Example, find all students who have first name of "Tom". We need to access each block of Student.

If the number of blocks of Student is 10000/20 or 500,

Reading Cost ($s_{firstName='Tom'}$ (Student)) = b(Student) = 500

Using Hash Key

- Suppose A is a hash key having unique values
- Apply the hashing algorithm to calculate the target address for the record
- For no overflow, the expected number of accesses is 1
- If overflow, need an estimate of the average number of accesses required to reach a record, depends on the amount of overflow and the overflow handling method
- This statistic, h, may be available to the optimizer
- cost is **h**

Example, suppose Faculty file is hashed on facId and h=2

Reading Cost ($s_{facId='F101'}$ (Faculty)) = 2

Index on Unique Key

- For index on a unique key field, retrieve index blocks and then go directly to the record from the index
- System stores the number of levels in indexes
- Cost is **I(index-name) + 1**

Example: $s_{stuId = 'S1001'}$ (Student)

Since stuId is the primary key, suppose index on stuId is called Student_stuId_ndx, and has 3 levels

Reading Cost ($s_{stuId='S1001'}$ (Student)) = I(Student_stuId_ndx) + 1 = 3+1 = 4

Non-clustered Index on a Secondary Key Attribute

- Suppose there is a non-clustering index on secondary key A
- Number of tuples that satisfy the condition is the selection size of the indexed attribute, s(A=c,R)
- Must assume the tuples are on different blocks
- Assume all the tuples having value A=c are pointed to by the index, perhaps using a linked list or an array of pointers
- Cost is the number of index accesses plus the number of blocks for the tuples that satisfy the condition, or
  I(index-name) + s(A=c,R)

Example, assume a non-clustering index on major in Student. For $s_{major='CSC'}$ (Student), find records having a major value of 'CSC' by reading the index node for 'CSC' and going from there to each tuple it points to. If the index has 2 levels, cost is

Reading Cost($s_{major='CSC'}$ (Student)) = I(Student_major_ndx) + s(major='SCS', Student)= 2 + (10000/25) = 2+400 = 402

- Note that this is only slightly less than the worst case cost, which is 500.

Selection Using a Clustered Index

- If we have a clustering index on A, use the selection size for A divided by the blocking factor to estimate the number of data blocks
- Assume the tuples of R having value A = c reside on contiguous blocks, so this calculation estimates the number of blocks needed to store these tuples
- We add that to the number of index blocks needed
- Cost is then **l(index-name) + (s(A=c,R))/bf(R))**
- Example, if the index on major in the Student file were a clustering index, we would assume that the 400 records expected to have this value for major would be stored on contiguous blocks and the index would point to the first block. Then we could simply retrieve the following blocks to find all 400 records. The cost is

Reading Cost(smajor='CSC' (Student)) = l(Student_major_ndx) + s(major='SCS', Student)/bf(Student) =2+400/20 = 22

Selection on an Ordered File

- A is a key with unique values and records are in order by A
- Use binary search to access the record with A value of c
- Cost is approximately $\log_2 b(R)$

Example, find a class record for a given classNumber, where Class file is in order by classNumber. Calculating the number of blocks in the table, if there are 2,500 Class records, each 100 bytes long, stored in blocks of size 4K, the blocking factor is 4096/100, or 40, so the number of blocks is 2500/40 or 63

Reading Cost($s_{classNumber='Eng201A'}$ (Class)) = $\log_2(63) \approx 6$

- If A is not a key, may be several records with A value of c. Estimate must consider the selection size, s(A=c,R) divided by the number of records per block.
- Cost is $\log_2 b(R) + s(A=c,R)/bf(R)$

Conjunctive Selection with a Composite Index

- If predicate is a conjunction and a composite index exists for the attributes in the predicate, this case reduces to one of the previous cases
- Cost depends on whether the attributes are a composite key, and whether the index is clustered

Conjunctive Selection without a Composite Index

- If one of the conditions involves an attribute which is used for ordering records in the file, or has an index or a hash key, then we use the appropriate method from those previously described to retrieve records that satisfy that part of the predicate, using the cost estimates given previously
- Once we retrieve the records we check to see if they satisfy the rest of the conditions
- If no attribute can be used for efficient retrieval, use the full table scan and check all the conditions simultaneously for each tuple

Processing Joins

- The join is generally the most expensive operation to perform in a relational system
- Since it is often used in queries, it is important to be able to estimate its cost
- Cost depends on the method of processing as well as the size of the results

Estimating Size of the Join Result-1

- Let R and S have size t(R) and t(S)
- If the tables have no common attributes, can only do a Cartesian product, and the number of tuples in the result is **t(R) * t(S)**
- If the set of common attributes is a key for one of the relations, the number of tuples in the join can be no larger than the number of tuples in the other relation, since each of these can match no more than one of the key values
- If the common attributes are a key for R, then the size of the join is **less than or equal to t(S)**

Ex. For natural join of Student and Enroll, since stuId is the primary key of Student, the number of tuples in the result will be the same as the number of tuples in Enroll, or 50,000, since each Enroll tuple has exactly one matching Student tuple

Notes

Estimating Size of the Join Result-2

- If common attributes are not a key of either relation
  - assume that there is one common attribute, A, whose values are uniformly distributed in both relations. For a particular value, c, of A in R, the number of tuples in S having a matching value of c for A is the selection size of A in S, or s(A=c,S), which is t(S)/n(A,S). This gives us the number of matches in S for a particular tuple in R. However, since there are t(R) tuples in R, each of which may have this number of matches, the total expected number of matches in the join is

  $$t(R \bowtie S) = t(R) * t(S) / n(A,S)$$

- If we had started by considering tuples in S and looked for matches in R, we would have derived $t(R \bowtie S) = t(S) * t(R) / n(A,R)$
- Use the formula that gives the smaller result

Cost of Writing Join Result

- Estimate the number of bytes in the joined tuples to be roughly the sum of the bytes of R and S, and divide the block size by that number to get the blocking factor of the result
- The number of blocks in the result is the expected number of tuples divided by the blocking factor

Methods of Performing Joins

- Nested loops-default method
- Sort-merge join
- Using index or hash key

Cost of Performing Nested Loop Joins

- Default method, used when no special access paths exist
- If we have two buffers for reading, plus one for writing the result, bring the first block of R into the first buffer, and then bring each block of S, in turn, into the second buffer
- Compare each tuple of the current R block with each tuple of the current S block before switching in the next S block
- Once finished all the S blocks, bring in the next R block into the first buffer, and go through all the S blocks again
- Repeat this process until all of R has been compared with all of S
- See Figure 11.5
- **Read cost (R |¥| S) = b(R) + (b(R)*b(S))**
since each block of R has to be read, and each block of S has to be read once for each block of R.

More on Nested Loop Joins

- Should pick the smaller file for the outside loop, since number of blocks in file in the outer loop file must be added to the product
- If buffer can hold more than three blocks, read as many blocks as possible from the outer loop file, and only one block from the inner loop file, plus one for writing the result
- If b(B) is the number of buffer blocks, using R as the outer loop, read b(B)-2 blocks of R into the buffer at a time, and 1 block of S
- Total number of R blocks still b(R), but number of S blocks is approximately b(S)*(b(R)/(b(B) - 2))
- The cost of accessing the files:
b(R) + ((b(S)*(b(R))/(b(B) - 2))

Nested Join with Small Files

- If all of R fits in main memory, with room for one block of S and one block for result, then read R only once, while switching in blocks of S one at a time
- The cost of reading the two packed files is then the most efficient possible cost
b(R) + b(S)

Sort-Merge Join

- If both files are sorted on the attribute(s) to be joined, the join algorithm is like the algorithm for merging two sorted files
- **b(R) + b(S)**
- If unsorted, may be worthwhile to sort files before a join
- Add the cost of sorting, which depends on the sorting method used

Join Using Index or Hash Key

- if A is a hash key for S, retrieve each tuple of R in the usual way, and use hashing algorithm to find all the matching records of S. Cost is

  b(R) + t(R)*h

- For index, cost depends on the type of index
- If A is the primary key of S, access cost is cost of accessing blocks of R plus cost of reading the index and accessing one record of S for each of the tuples in R

  b(R) + (t(R) * (I(indexname) + 1))

- If A is not a primary key, consider the number of matches in S per tuple of R, **b(R) + (t(R) * (I(indexname) + s(A=c,S)))**
- If the index is a clustering index, reduce the estimate by dividing by the blocking factor

  b(R) + (t(R) * (I(indexname) + s(A=c,S)/bf(S))

Cost of Projection with Key

- Projection requires finding the values of the attributes in the projection list for each tuple, and eliminating duplicates, if any
- If the projection list contains a key of the relation, there are no duplicates to eliminate
  - The read cost is number of blocks in the relationis

    b(R)
  - The number of tuples in the result is number of tuples in the relation, t(R)
  - The resulting tuples may be much smaller than the tuples of R, so the number of blocks needed to write the result may be much smaller than b(R)

Cost of Projection-General Case

- If the projection list does not contain key, must eliminate duplicates
- Method Using Sorting
  - Sort the results so that duplicates appear together
  - eliminate any tuple that is a duplicate of the previous one
  - Cost is the sum of the costs of
    - Accessing all the blocks of the relation to create a temporary file with only attributes on the projection list
    - Writing the temporary file
    - Sorting the temporary file
    - Accessing the sorted temporary file to eliminate duplicates
    - Writing the final results file
  - Most expensive step is sorting temporary file
    - Use external sorting since DB files are large
    - Can use two-way merge sort can be used if there are 3 buffers available
    - if file has n pages, the number of passes needed will be (log$_2$n)+1, and the number of disk accesses required just for the sorting phase will be
    - **2n((log$_2$n)+1))**
- Can use hashing method if several buffers available

Cost of Set Operations

- Sort both files on the same attributes
- Use basic sort-merge algorithm
  - For union, put in results file any tuple that appears in either of the original files, but drop duplicates
  - For intersection, place in the results file only the tuples that appear in both of the original files, but drop duplicates
  - For set difference, R - S, examine each tuple of R and place it in the results file if it has no match in S
- Cost is the sum of the cost of
  - Accessing all the blocks of both files
  - Sorting both and writing the temporary sorted files
  - Accessing the temporary files to do the merge
  - Writing the results file

Pipelining

- Materialization of intermediate results can be expensive
- **pipelining**
  - tuples "pass through" from one operation to the next in the pipeline, without creation of a temporary file
  - cannot be used in algorithms that require that the entire relation as input

Notes

Databases Illuminated

Databases Illuminated
Catherine Ricardo

Chapter 12
Distributed Databases

Distributed Database System

- Multiple sites connected by a communications system
- Data at any site available to users at other sites
- Sites may be far apart; linked by telecommunications lines
- May be close together; linked by a local area network

Advantages of Distribution

- Compared to a single, centralized system that provides remote access, distributed system advantages are
  - Local autonomy
  - Improved reliability
  - Better data availability
  - Increased performance
  - Reduced response time
  - Lower communications costs

Notes

Architecture Design Considerations

- Factors the designer considers in choosing an architecture for a distributed system
  - Type of communications system
  - Data models supported
  - Types of applications
  - Data placement alternatives

Architecture Alternatives

- Centralized database with distributed processing
- Client-server system
- Parallel databases
  - Shared memory
  - Shared disk
  - Shared nothing
  - Cluster
- true distributed database-data and processing shared among autonomous sites

Types of Distributed Systems

- **Homogeneous**
  - All nodes use the same hardware and software
- **Heterogeneous**
  - Nodes have different hardware or software
  - Require translations of codes and word lengths due to hardware differences
  - Translation of data models and data structures due to software differences

Software Components of DDBMS

- Data communications component (DC)
- Local database management system (DBMS)
- Global data dictionary (GDD)
- Distributed database management system component (DDBMS)
- Not all sites have all these components

DDBMS Functions

- Provides the user interface
  - Needed for location transparency
- Locates the data
  - Directs queries to proper site(s)
- Processes queries
  - Local, remote, compound (global)
- Provides network-wide concurrency control and recovery procedures
- Provides translation in heterogeneous systems

Data Placement Alternatives

- Centralized
  - All data at one site only
- Replicated
  - All data duplicated at all sites
- Partitioned
  - Data divided among sites
  - Fragmentation scheme: horizontal, vertical, mixed fragments
  - Each item appears only once
- Hybrid
  - Combination of the others

Factors in Data Placement Decision

- Locality of reference
- Reliability of data
- Availability of data
- Storage capacities and costs
- Distribution of processing load
- Communications costs

Types of Transparency

- Data distribution transparency
  - Fragmentation transparency
  - Location transparency
  - Replication transparency
- DBMS heterogeneity transparency
- Transaction transparency
  - Concurrency transparency
  - Recovery transparency
- Performance transparency

Transaction Management for DDBMS

- Each site that initiates transactions has a **transaction coordinator** to manage transactions that originate there
  - For local or remote transactions, transaction manager at data site takes over
  - For global transactions, originating site coordinator
    - Starts execution
    - Uses GDD to form subtransactions
    - Directs subtransactions to appropriate sites
    - Receives subtransaction results
    - Controls transaction end-either commit or abort at all sites
- Additional concurrency control problem
  - **Multiple-copy inconsistency** problem
- Solutions use **locking** and **timestamping**

Locking Protocols

- Extension of two-phase locking protocol
  - Single-site lock manager
    - May use Read-One-Write-All replica handling
    - Site may become a bottleneck
  - Distributed lock manager
    - Can use Read-One-Write-All method
    - Deadlock difficult to determine
  - Primary copy
    - Dominant node for each data item
  - Majority locking

Global Deadlock Detection

- Each site has local wait-for graph-detects only local deadlock
- Need global wait-for graph
  - Single site can be global deadlock detection coordinator
  - Constructs global graph and checks for cycles
  - Responsibility could be shared among sites

Timestamping Protocols

- One site could issue all timestamps
- Instead, multiple sites could issue them
  - Each timestamp has two parts-the time and the node identifier
  - Guarantees uniqueness of timestamps
  - Difficult to synchronize clocks-to control divergence, can advance clock reading if later timestamp received
  - Can apply basic timestamping, Thomas' Write Rule, multiversion timestamp protocols using unique timestamps

Recovery-Failures

- Must guarantee atomicity and durability of transactions
- Failures include usual types, plus loss of messages, site failure, link failure
- Network partitioning
  - Failure where network splits into groups of nodes that are isolated from other groups, but can communicate with one another

Handling Node Failure

- System flags node as failed
- System aborts and rolls back affected transactions
- System checks periodically to see if node has recovered, or node self-reports
- After restart, failed node does local recovery
- Failed node catches up to current state of DB, using system log of changes made while it was unavailable

Commit Protocols

- Two-phase commit protocl
  - Phase 1-voting phase
    - Coordinator writes <begin commit T> to its log, writes log to disk, sends <prepare T> msg to all participants. Each site either does a <ready T> or <abort T> and sends its vote to coordinator
  - Phase 2-resolution phase
    - Coordinator resolves fate of transaction
      - If any abort msg received, makes all sites abort
      - Failure of any site to vote generates global abort
      - If all sites voted ready, coordinator tells all to commit
      - Handles various types of failure
- Three-phase commit protocol – non-blocking, assumes no more than k sites fail, for some k

Distributed Query Processing

- Queries can be
  - local: done at originating site only
  - Remote: done at different site
  - Compound: requires multiple sites
- Must consider cost of transferring data between sites
- Semijoin operation is sometimes used when a join of data stored at different sites is required

Steps in Distributed Query-1

1. Accept user's request
2. Check request's validity
3. Check user's authorization
4. Map external to logical level
5. Determine request processing strategy
6. For heterogeneous system, translate query to DML of data node(s)
7. Encrypt request
8. Determine routing (job of DC component)

Steps in Distributed Query-2

9. Transmit messages (job of DC component)
10. Each node decrypts its request
11. Do update synchronization
12. Each data node's local DBMS does its processing
13. Nodes translate data, if heterogeneous system
14. Nodes send results to requesting node or other destination node
15. Consolidate results, edit, format results
16. Return results to user

Chapter 13: Databases and the Internet

chapter 13

Notes

Databases Illuminated

Catherine Ricardo

Databases Illuminated

Chapter 13
Databases and the Internet

Databases and the WWW

- WWW is a loosely organized information resource
- Many websites use static linked HTML files
  - can become inconsistent and outdated
- Many organizations provide dynamic access to databases directly from the Web
- Dynamic database access from Web introduces new problems for designers and DBAs

Uses for Web-based DB Applications

- e-commerce has pushed organizations to develop Web-based database applications
  - To create world-wide markets
  - To deliver information
  - To provide better customer service
  - To communicate with their suppliers
  - To provide training for employees
  - To expand the workplace
  - ...Many other innovative activities

Databases and the Internet

131

Origins of The Internet

- Developed from **Arpanet**, communications network created in the 1960s by DARPA, US agency, for linking government and academic research institutions
- Used a common protocol, **TCP/IP**
- US National Science Foundation took over management of the network, then referred to as the **Internet**
- Navigating and using the Internet required considerable sophistication

World Wide Web

- Tim Berners-Lee proposed a method of simplifying access to Internet resources in 1989
- Led to the development of the **World Wide Web**
- included notions of **URL, HTTP, HTML, hypertext, graphical browsers** with **links**
- Automated finding, downloading, and displaying files on the Internet

URL

- Specific type of **Uniform Resource Identifier** (URI)
  - String giving the location of any type of resource on the Internet-Web pages, mailboxes, downloadable files, etc.

HTTP

- Communications protocol
  - Standard for structure of messages
- HTTP is a **stateless** protocol
  - No facility for remembering previous interactions
  - Creates a problem for e-commerce, which requires a continuous session with the user

HTML

- Data format used for presenting content on the Internet
- A **markup** language because HTML documents contain tags that provide formatting information for the text
- HTML document can contain applets, audio files, images, video files, content

XML

- Extensible Markup Language - standard for document storage, exchange, and retrieval
- Created in 1996 by the World Wide Web Consortium (W3) XML Special Interest Group
- Users can define their own markup language, including their own tags that describe data items in documents, including databases
- Can define the structure of heterogeneous databases and support translation of data between different databases

Components of XML Documents

- **Element** is the basic component of an XML document
- Document contains one or more XML elements, each of which has a **start tag** showing the name of the element, some **character data**, and an **end tag**
- Can be **subelements** of other elements- must be properly nested
- Can have **attributes** whose names and values are shown inside the element's start tag
- Attributes occur only once within each element, while subelements can occur any number of times
- Document can contain **entity references**-refer to external files, common text, Unicode characters, or reserved symbols

Well-Formed XML Document

- Obey rules of XML
  - Starts with XML declaration
  - Root element contains all other elements
  - All elements properly nested

DTD and XML Schema

- Users can define their own markup language by writing either
  - A **Document Type Declaration** (DTD)
    - A specification for a set of rules for the elements, attributes, and entities of a document
    - A document that obeys the rules of its associated DTD is **type-valid**
  - An **XML Schema**
    - New, more powerful way to describe the structure of documents
    - A document that conforms to an XML schema is **schema-valid**

DTD Rules

- DTD is enclosed in <!DOCTYPE *name[DTDdeclaration]*>
- each **element** is declared using a type declaration with structure <!ELEMENT (*content type*)>
- In an element declaration, the name of any subelement can be followed by one of the symbols *, + or ?, to indicate the number of times the subelement occurs
- **Attribute** list declarations for elements are declared outside the element

XML Schema

- Permits more complex structure than DTD
- Additional fundamental data types, UDTs
- User-created domain vocabulary
- Supports uniqueness and foreign key constraints
- Schema lists elements and attributes
  - Elements may be complex, which means they have subelements, or simple
  - elements can occur multiple times
  - Attributes or elements can be used to store data values
  - Attributes used for simple values that are not repeated

Three-tier Architecture

- Three major functions required in an Internet environment: presentation, application logic, data management
- Placement of functions depends on architecture of system
- **Three tier architectures** completely separate application logic from data management
  - Client handles the user interface, the **presentation layer** or first tier
  - **Application server** executes the application logic -the **middle tier**
  - **Database server** forms the third tier
- Communications network connects each tier to the next

Advantages of 3-tier Architecture

- Allows support for **thin clients** that only handle the presentation layer
- Independence of tiers; may use different platforms
- Easier application maintenance on the application server
- Integrated transparent data access to heterogeneous data sources
- Scalability

Presentation Layer

- **HTML forms** often used at the presentation layer
- Scripting languages such as Perl, JavaScript, JScript, VBScript, may be embedded in HTML to provide some client-side processing
- **Style sheets** specify how data is presented on specific devices

Application Server

- Middle tier - responsible for executing applications
  - Determines the flow of control
  - Acquires input data from presentation layer
  - Makes data requests to database server
  - Accepts query results from database layer
  - Uses them to assemble dynamically generated HTML pages
- Server-side processing can use different technologies such as Java Servlets, Java Server pages, etc.
- **CGI**, Common Gateway Interface, can be used to connect HTML forms with application programs
- To maintain state during a session, servers may use cookies, hidden fields in HTML forms, and URI extensions.
  - Cookies generated at the middle tier using Java's Cookie class, sent to the client, where they are stored in the browser cache

Data Layer

- Third layer is standard database or other data source
- Ideally on separate server

XML and Semi-structured Data Model

- Semistructured data model uses a tree structure
- Nodes represent **complex objects** or **atomic values**
- An **edge** represents either relationship between an object and its sub-object, or between an object and its value
- Leaf nodes, with no sub-objects, represent values
- Nodes of the graph for a structured XML document are ordered using **pre-order traversal**, depth-first, left-to-right order
- There is no separate schema, since the graph is self-describing

Queries

- **XQuery** is W3C standard query language for XML data
  - Uses the abstract logical structure of a document as it is encoded in XML
  - Queries use a path expression, which comes from an earlier language, **XPath**
  - Consists of the document name and specification of the elements to be retrieved, using a path relationship
  - Can add conditions to any nodes in a path expression
  - Evaluated by reading forward in the document until a node of the specified type and condition is encountered

FLOWR Expressions

- XQuery uses a **FLWOR** expression::FOR, LET, WHERE, ORDER BY, and RETURN clauses
- Ex
  FOR $C IN doc("CustomerList.xml")//Customer)
  WHERE $C/Type="Individual"
  ORDER BY Name
  RETURN <Result> $N/Name, $N/Status </Result>

- Allows for binding of variables to results
- Allows for iterating through the nodes of a document
- Allows joins to be performed
- Allows data to be restructured
- XQuery provides many predefined functions, including count, avg, max, min, and sum, which can be used in FLOWR expressions.

XML and Relational Databases

- Relational DBMSs extended their native datatypes to allow storage of XML documents
- Also possible to use SQL with XPath expressions to retrieve values from the database
- Existing heterogeneous databases can be queried using standard languages such as SQL, and query results can be placed into an XML instance document
- Query language has to have facilities that can tag and structure relational data into XML format

Notes

Databases Illuminated

Chapter 14
Social and Ethical Issues

Computerization and Ethical Issues

- New temptations due to computer technology-factors (according to Richard Rubin)
  - Speed
  - Privacy
  - Anonymity
  - Ease of copying
  - Aesthetic attraction
  - Availability of potential victims
  - International scope
  - The power to destroy

Ethical Challenges and the Internet

- The Internet largely unregulated
  - Not subject to the rules of any single country
  - Its culture resists regulation
  - Forum for free speech, but can lead to abuses such as pornography and hate rhetoric
  - Disagreements about intellectual property rights
- Need to understand intellectual property protection both for Internet and database content and for software-both sides of issues
- Need to understand privacy rights and their protection

Notes

Intellectual Property

- Sir William Blackstone: "Blackstonian bundle" of property rights
  - Right to use as owner sees fit
  - To receive income from it
  - To transfer ownership
  - To exclude others from it
- **Intellectual property** refers to products of the mind, such as literature, music, art, architecture, inventions, formulas for products, and software
- One definition: "the legal rights which result from intellectual activity in the industrial, scientific, literary and artistic fields" (WIPO)
- The foundation is that the creator of an original work has invested time and resources, and is entitled to a just return, which in turn encourages creative people to develop new works

Legal Protections

- Copyright
- Patent
- Trade secret
- Trademarks and service marks.

Nature of Copyright

- Given by the government of the country of origin for a limited period
- Author has exclusive rights to make copies, publish, distribute, publicly display, or publicly perform the work or to use it as the basis of a derivative work during that period
- Work must be original, have a tangible form, and be fixed in a medium
- Facts, ideas, and formulas are always in the public domain, but a specific arrangement and expression of them, such as that found in a database, can be copyrighted
- Creator automatically owns the copyright, even without publication, copyright symbol, or formal registration
- Except for personal use, anyone who wants to use the copyrighted work must obtain permission from the owner, unless the use is "fair use"

Fair Use

- Limited non-personal use of copyrighted materials, including using a small amount for educational purposes, and similar uses
- Four factors to be considered
  - Character of the use
  - Nature of the work
  - Amount of the work to be used
  - Effect on the market for the original work

Copyright Law

- Each country makes its own laws concerning copyright; most based on the Berne Convention
- Copyrights are recognized internationally
- In the US
  - Works created before 1978 copyrighted for 95 years
  - Post-1978 works are copyrighted for the lifetime of the author plus 70 years; but works for hire 95 or 120 years.
  - Copyright law covers software, both source code and object code
  - 1998 The Digital Millennium Copyright Act
    - Controversial provisions on tools designed to circumvent protection or encryption systems; a crime to use, manufacture or offer such a tool
    - Exceptions
      - for libraries, archives, and educational institutions, only for evaluating the work
      - for law enforcement agencies
      - for reverse engineering to allow interoperability of products
      - for encryption research
      - for computer repairs, and similar uses.
    - limits the liability of Internet service providers for online copyright infringement by subscribers

Patents

- Grant of a property right to an inventor
- Issued by governments of individual countries, but Paris Convention allows inventor to patent in other countries, using same date as original
- Gives inventor the right to prevent others from making, using, offering to sell, selling, or importing the invention
- Term generally 20 years, to recover costs of creating invention
- Invention must be "useful", new, and non-obvious
- Inventor must file an application with a specification, describing the invention in detail
- US Patent office sends details to a technology center for examination
- Patent number, "Patent pending" and "patent applied for" warn others of patent

Trade Secrets

- Any information that is used in the operation of a business that is kept secret and that gives it a competitive edge
- In US, trade secrets are protected by states, but there is a Uniform Trade Secrets Act among states
- Laws protect the company from misappropriation of the secret
- Protection remains as long as the information is kept secret
- Factors that courts use in determining a trade secret
  - How widely the information is known both outside and inside
  - Extent of measures taken to guard its secrecy
  - Value of the information to the owner and the competitors
  - Amount of time, effort and money spent in developing it
  - How difficult it would be for others to duplicate it properly

Trademarks and Service Marks

- Marks also eligible for protection under intellectual protection laws
- Can include letters, numbers, words, drawings, symbols, colors, sounds, fragrances, or shape or packaging of goods that are distinctive
- In US, protected by federal law under Lanham Act
- In US, register marks with US Patent Office and Trademark Office
- Madrid Protocol-international registration-also WIPO

Software Protection

- Software and its packaging can be protected by copyright, by patent or trade secret laws, by trademark, or by some combination of these
- Customer who buys software is actually buying a license to use the software, not the software itself, which remains the property of the owner
- Open source software is free and available for copying. See
  - Free Software Foundation-Richard Stallman, President
  - "The Cathedral and the Bazaar"-Eric Raymond
- Shareware which allows people to download and use the software for an evaluation period, after which they should pay for its continued use

Notes

Database Protection

- Commercial DBMS usually protected with same intellectual property protections as other software
- Custom applications written for a database also qualify for software protections
- Databases qualified for different kinds of protection
  - Database can be copyrighted, because it is an expression
  - Facts contained in the database cannot be copyrighted
  - Information in a database can also be treated as a trade secret, since it can be used to provide a competitive advantage

Privacy Issues

- Databases make it possible to store massive amounts of data about individuals
- Data matching and communication technologies can compile and share information about individuals without their knowledge or consent
- Whether it is ethical to collect certain data about an individual, to use it without the consent of the individual, and to share it with third parties are the subject of much debate
- US and EU practices differ significantly
- Conflict between the individual's right to privacy and the desire of governments and businesses to have information that would be useful to them

Privacy Rights

- Privacy recognized as a fundamental human right
  - Enshrined in the constitutions of many countries
  - Declaration of Human Rights by the United Nations
  - Conventions adopted by the European Council
  - Laws enacted in the US and other countries
- US laws generally based on Fair Information Practices, from 1972 HEW report

Notes

US Privacy Laws Concerning Government Activites

- The Freedom of Information Act, 1966
- The Privacy Act of 1974
  - Banned use of social security numbers as universal identifiers
  - Four policies for government agencies
    - Restrict disclosure of personally identifiable records
    - Grant people right to access their records
    - Grant right to seek amendment of their records
    - Conform to Fair Information Practices
- The Computer Matching and Privacy Protection Act, 1990
- The Patriot Act of 2002 weakened the provisions of some of these privacy laws, in the interests of national security

US Privacy Laws Concerning Business Activities

- Individual laws were passed to deal with practices in various business sectors
- Some examples
  - Fair Credit Reporting Act of 1970
  - Right to Financial Privacy Act of 1978
  - Cable Privacy Protection Act of 1984
  - Electronic Communication Privacy Act of 1986
  - Video Privacy Protection Act of 1988
  - Telephone Consumer Protection Act of 1991
  - Health Insurance Portability and Accountability Act of 1996
  - Gramm Leach Bliley Financial Services Modernization Act of 1999
- Generally they require that consumers have to **opt-out** to prevent their information from being shared

Privacy Protection in EU Countries

- European laws are more restrictive of business activities.
- Require "opt-in" rather than "opt-out" as the mechanism for obtaining customer approval of data sharing
- Based on principles developed by the Organization of Economic Cooperation and Development (OECD)
- Principles of
  - Collection limitation
  - Data quality
  - Purpose specification
  - Use limitation
  - Security safeguards
  - Openness
  - Individual participation
  - Accountability.

EU Privacy Principles-1

- **Collection Limitation Principle**.
  - limits to the collection of personal data
  - Be obtained by lawful and fair means
  - Be collected with the knowledge or consent of the subject
- **Data Quality Principle**. Personal data should be
  - Relevant to the purposes
  - Collected only to the extent necessary
  - Accurate, complete and up-to-date.
- **Purpose Specification Principle**.
  - Purposes should be specified in advance of data collection
  - Not used again except for fulfilling those purposes
- **Use Limitation Principle**. Personal data should not be shared or used for purposes other than those stated in the Purpose Specification principle except with the consent of the subject or by the authority of law.

EU Privacy Principles-2

- **Security Safeguards Principle**. Reasonable security measures to protect personal data against unauthorized access, use, disclosure, modification, destruction, and loss.
- **Openness Principle**. There should be a general policy of openness -should be easily possible to know about its existence, nature, purpose of use, and the name and contact information of the person who controls it (called the **data controller**).
- **Individual Participation Principle**. An individual should be able to
  - Find out whether the data controller has data relating to him or her
  - Find out what that data is within a reasonable time, at a reasonable charge (if any), and in a form that is understandable.
  - Challenge the denial of any such request and to challenge data related to him or her. If the challenge is successful, the individual has the right to have the data corrected or erased.
- **Accountability Principle**. A data controller should be accountable for complying with the principles

US vs EU Rules

- Data about EU citizens must be afforded the same level of protection when it leaves the country.
- US companies doing business in EU countries had problems obtaining the data needed for their business, since they could not legally obtain customer information from those countries
- US companies can certify that they follow the rules of the **Safe Harbor** agreement, which means that they comply with the EU rules in the way they treat data, and can receive such data

Human Factors

- Refer to physical and psychological factors that promote or facilitate optimal performance on the part of the user
- User-centered design increases user comfort, safety, productivity, and satisfaction, and reduces training costs and errors
- includes consideration of the user at every stage of the system project
- Five components of usability are
  - Learnability
  - Efficiency
  - Memorability
  - Error reduction
  - Satisfaction
- Repeated testing at each stage improves usability

Professional Standards

- ACM Code of Ethics and Professional Conduct

www.acm.org/constitution/code.html

- ACM/IEEE Software Engineering Code of Ethics and Professional Practices

www.computer.org/tab/seprof/code.htm

Notes

Databases Illuminated

Catherine Ricardo

Databases Illuminated

Chapter 15
Data Warehouses and Data Mining

Intro to Data Warehouses

- Term coined by W.H. Inmon
  - "a subject-oriented, integrated, non-volatile, time-varying collection of data that is used primarily in organizational decision making"
- Enterprises use historical and current data taken from operational databases as resource for decision making
- Data warehouses store massive amounts of data
- Typical uses
  - decision support systems (DSS)
  - on-line analytical processing (OLAP)
  - data mining
- Major DB vendors provide warehouse features, including analytical tools
- SQL:1999 includes data mining functions

Characteristics of Operational Databases

- Support online transaction processing (OLTP)
  - use limited number of repetitive transactions
  - transactions involve a few tuples at a time
- Serve the information needs of end users
- Support day-to-day business operations
- Require high availability and efficient performance
- Handle large volume of transactions
- Must deliver query responses quickly
- Must do updates quickly
- State must reflect current environment of the enterprise

Notes

Characteristics of Data Warehouses

- Support **on-line analytical processing- OLAP**
  - Examine large amounts of data to produce results
  - Allow complex queries, often using grouping
  - Support time-series analysis using historical data
- Used for decision making
- Contain very large amount of data
- Have data from multiple operational databases, taken at different periods of time (historical data)
- Sources may have different models or standards; data warehouse integrates the data
- May include data from other sources, summarized data, metadata
- Optimized for efficient query processing and presentation of results
- Updates done periodically; not in real time
- Support **data mining-**discovering new information by searching large amounts of data
  - purpose is to discover patterns or trends in the data

Data Warehouse Architecture-1

- See Figure 15.1
- Must support ad-hoc queries and unanticipated types of analysis
- Input data
  - Taken from various data sources
    - Multiple operational databases
    - Independent files
    - Environmental data-e.g.geographical or financial data
  - Extracted using back-end system tools-accommodate differences among heterogeneous sources
  - Reformatted into a consistent form
  - Checked for integrity and validity- **data cleaning**
  - Put into the data model for the warehouse
  - Loaded - long transaction due to large volume

Data Warehouse Architecture-2

- DBMS for data warehouse has
  - System catalog that stores metadata
  - Other standard database system components
- **Data marts** - segments of the data organized into subsets that focus on specific subjects; e.g. may contain specialized information about a single department
- Data warehouse output
  - Supports queries for OLAP
  - Provides information for decision support systems
  - Provides data for data mining tools
  - Can result in new knowledge, which can then be used as a data source

Data Refresh

- Data from all sources must be refreshed periodically
- New data is added to the existing warehouse, if there is room; old data is kept as long as it is useful
- Data no longer used is purged periodically
- Frequency and scope of updates depends on the environment
- Factors for deciding the update policy
  - How much storage is available
  - Whether the warehouse needs recent data
  - Whether warehouse can be off-line during refresh
  - How long the process of transmitting the data, cleaning, formatting, loading, and building indexes will take
- usual policy is to do a partial refresh periodically

Data Models for Data Warehouses

- Generally use a multidimensional model
- **Data cube** - multidimensional matrix for storing data
  - Can view the data by dimension of interest
  - Possible operations on data cube
    - **pivoting** - rotating to display a different dimension
    - **rollup** - displaying a coarser level of data granularity, by combining or aggregating data
    - **drill-down** - showing more detail on some dimension, using finer granularity for the data; requires that the more detailed data be available
    - **slicing** - examining a portion of the data cube using a selection with equality conditions for one or more dimensions; appears as if the user has cut through the cube in the selected directions
    - **dicing** - specifying a range of values in a selection
    - **Cross-tabulation** – displaying totals for the rows and columns in a two-dimensional spreadsheet-style display
- **Hypercube** - data cube of dimension > 3
  - Possible to do pivoting, rollup, drilling down, slicing, dicing
  - No physical representation of cube itself

Schemas for Data Warehouses

- **Multidimensional OLAP (MOLAP)** systems use multidimensional arrays
- **Relational OLAP (ROLAP)** systems use relational model
- **ROLAP warehouse** has multiple relational tables
- **Star schema**
  - Central **fact table** of unaggregated, observed data
  - Has attributes that represent dimensions, plus dependent attributes
  - Each dimension has its own dimension table
  - Dimension tables have corresponding dimension attributes in fact table, usually foreign keys there
- **Snowflake schema**
  - Variation in which normalized dimension tables have dimensions themselves
- See Figure 15.4

Warehouse Queries in SQL92 Form

- SQL92 aggregate functions SUM, COUNT, MAX, MIN and AVG allow some slicing and dicing queries. Form is

```
SELECT <grouping attributes> <aggregation function>
FROM <fact table> JOIN <dimension table(s)>
WHERE <attribute = constant>... <attribute = constant>
GROUP BY <grouping attributes>;
```

SQL:1999 Warehouse Queries

- SQL:1999 includes functions for
  - **stddev** (standard deviation) and **variance** for single attributes – measures of data spread from mean
  - **correlation** and **regression**, which apply to pairs of attributes
  - **rank** for data values
  - GROUP BY extended with CUBE and ROLLUP options

Indexes for Warehouses

- Efficient indexes important because of large quantity of data
- Allow queries to be executed in reasonable time
- Since data is relatively static, cost of maintaining indexes is not a factor
- Special indexing techniques used for warehouses
  - bitmap indexing
  - join indexing

Bitmap Indexes

- Can be constructed for any attributes that have a limited number of distinct possible values-small domain
- For each value in the domain, a bit vector is constructed to represent that value, by placing a 1 in the position for that value
- Take much less space than standard indexes
- Allow processing of some queries directly from the index

Join Indexes

- Join is slow when tables are large
- Join indexes speed up join queries
- Most join operations are done on foreign keys
- For a star schema, the join operation involves comparing the fact table with dimension tables
- **Join index** relates the values of a dimension table to the rows of the fact table
- For each value of the indexed attribute in the dimension table, join index stores the tuple IDs of all the tuples in the fact table having that value

Views and Query Modification

- Views are important in data warehouses for customizing the user's environment
- SQL operators, including CUBE and ROLLUP, can be performed on views as well as on base tables
- SQL CREATE VIEW command defines the view, but does not create any new tables
- Can execute a query for a view by **query modification**, replacing the reference in the WHERE line by the view definition
- Query modification may be too slow in a warehouse environment

View Materialization

- View materialization – precomputing views from the definition and storing them for later use
- Indexes can be created for the materialized views, to speed processing of view queries
- Designer must decide which views to materialize; weighs storage constraints against benefit of speeding up important queries

Materialized View Maintenance

- When the underlying base tables change, view should also be updated
- **Immediate view maintenance**, done as part of the update transaction for the base tables; slows down the refresh transaction for the data warehouse
- Alternative is **deferred view maintenance**. Possible policies
  - **Lazy refresh**, update the view when a query using the view is executed and the current materialized version is obsolete
  - **Periodic refresh**, update the view at regular time intervals
  - **Forced refresh**, update the view after a specified number of updates to the underlying base tables
- Process can be done by recomputing the entire materialized view
- For complex views especially with joins or aggregations, may be done incrementally, incorporating only changes to the underlying tables

Data Mining

- Discovering new information from very large data sets
- Knowledge discovered is usually in the form of patterns or rules
- Uses techniques from statistics and artificial intelligence
- Need a large database or a data warehouse

Notes

Data Formats for Data Mining

- Data mining application should be considered in the original design of the warehouse
- Operations used in data mining differ from the analytical ones for OLAP and decision support systems
- Requires summarized data as well as raw data taken from original data sources
- Requires knowledge of the domain and of the data mining process
- Best data format is a "flat file" in which all the data for each case of observed values appears as a single record
- If "flat file" not used, data must be prepared and reformatted for data mining

Purpose of Data Mining

- Usually the ultimate purpose is to provide knowledge that will give a company a competitive advantage, enabling it to earn a greater profit
- Goals of data mining
  - Predict the future behavior of attributes
  - Classify items, placing them in the proper categories
  - Identify the existence of an activity or an event
  - Optimize the use of the organization's resources

Types of Knowledge Discovered

- Data mining uses **induction**
- Examines a large number of cases and concludes that a pattern or a rule exists
- Knowledge can be represented as rules, decision trees, neural networks, or frames

Possible Output: Association and Classification Rules

- **Association rules** have form {x} fi{y}, where x and y are events that occur at the same time.
  - Have measures of **support** and **confidence**.
    - Support is the percentage of transactions that contain all items included in both left and right hand sides
    - Confidence is how often the rule proves to be true; where the left hand side of the implication is present, percentage of those in which the right hand side is present as well
- **Classification rules,** placing instances into the correct one of several possible categories
  - Developed using a **training set,** past instances for which the correct classification is known
  - System develops a method for correctly classifying a new item whose class is currently unknown

Possible Output: Sequential Patterns

- **Sequential patterns** e.g. prediction that a customer who buys a particular product in one transaction will purchase a related product in a later transaction
  - Can involve a set of products
  - Patterns are represented as sequences {S1}, {S2}
  - First subsequence {S1} is a **predictor** of the second subsequence {S2}
  - **Support** is the percentage of times such a sequence occurs in the set of transactions
  - **Confidence** is the probability that when {S1} occurs, {S2} will occur on a subsequent transaction - can calculate from observed data

Time Series Patterns

- A **time series** is a sequence of events that are all of the same type
- Sales figures, stock prices, interest rates, inflation rates, and many other quantities can be analyzed using time series
- Time series data can be studied to discover patterns and sequences
- For example, we can look at the data to find the longest period when the figures continued to rise each month, or find the steepest decline from one month to the next

Data Mining Methods

- **Decision tree**, a method of developing classification rules
- Developed by examining past data to determine how significant attributes and values are related to outcomes
  - Nodes of the tree represent **partitioning attributes**, which allow the set of training instances to be partitioned into disjoint classes
  - The **partitioning conditions** are shown on the branches
- Tree is then used to classify new cases
- See Figure 15.6

Regression

- A statistical method for predicting the value of an attribute, Y, (the dependent variable), given the values of attributes X1, X2, ..., Xn (the independent variables)
- Statistical packages allow users to identify potential factors for predicting the value of the dependent variable
- Using **linear regression**, the package finds the contribution or weight of each independent variable, as coefficients, a0, a1, ..., an for a linear function $Y = a0 + a1\,X1 + a2\,X2 + \ldots + anXn$
- Formula represents a curve that fits the observed values as closely as possible.
- In data mining, system itself may be asked to identify the independent variables, as well as to find the regression function
- Can also use **non-linear regression**, using **curve-fitting**, finding the equation of the curve that fits the observed values

Neural Networks

- Methods from AI using a set of samples to find the strongest relationships between variables and observations
- Network given training set that provides facts about input values
- Use a learning method, adapting as they learn new information from additional samples
- Hidden layers developed by the system as it examines cases, using generalized regression technique
- System refines its hidden layers until it has learned to predict correctly a certain percentage of the time; then test cases are provided to evaluate it
- One problem: **overfitting** the curve - prediction function fits the training set values too perfectly, even ones that are incorrect (data noise); prediction function will then perform poorly on new data
- Knowledge of how the system makes its predictions is in the hidden layers: users do not see the reasoning; weights assigned to the factors cannot be interpreted in a natural way
- Output may be difficult to understand and interpret

Clustering

- Methods used to place cases into clusters or groups that can be disjoint or overlapping
- Using a training set, system identifies a set of clusters into which the tuples of the database can be grouped
- Tuples in each cluster are similar, and they are dissimilar to tuples in other clusters
- Similarity is measured by using a **distance function** defined for the data

Applications of Data Mining

- Retailing
  - Customer relations management (CRM)
  - Advertising campaign management
- Banking and Finance
  - Credit scoring
  - Fraud detection and prevention
- Manufacturing
  - Optimizing use of resources
  - Manufacturing process optimization
  - Product design
- Medicine
  - Determining effectiveness of treatments
  - Analyzing effects of drugs
  - Finding relationships between patient care and outcomes